Strange Design

*Exploring the ways of God
in the world*

Philip Crowe was formerly Rector of Overton, Erbistock and Penley in the diocese of St Asaph. He has served for twenty-four years in parish ministry, and has taught in three theological colleges, including six years as Principal of Salisbury and Wells College. He has contributed frequently to Radio 2 and Radio 4, and is a regular speaker on *Good Morning Wales*. He is currently Director of the St Asaph and Bangor Ministerial Training Course, and is a full-time gardener.

Strange Design

*Exploring the ways of God
in the world*

Philip Crowe

Foreword by
Bishop Rowan Williams

CANTERBURY
PRESS

Norwich

© Philip Crowe 1999

First published in 1999 by The Canterbury Press Norwich
(a publishing imprint of Hymns Ancient & Modern Limited
a registered charity)
St Mary's Works, St Mary's Plain
Norwich, Norfolk, NR3 3BH

British Library Cataloguing in Publication Data

A catalogue record for this book is available
from the British Library

ISBN 1-85311-326-3

Typeset by Rowland Phototypesetting,
Bury St Edmunds, Suffolk
Printed in Great Britain by
Biddles Ltd, Guildford and King's Lynn

Contents

Foreword

What does it mean to believe that God is in charge of the world? It is all too easy to understand this in terms of what we usually mean if we claim that *we* are in charge of something: the master-plan is in my head and I am bending circumstances to my will. But if God is bending circumstances to God's will, the world doesn't seem to give us a very promising picture of what that will might be.

It is one of the oldest riddles of theology and Philip Crowe's book helps us encounter it not as a theoretical question with a theoretical solution, but in terms of the daily anxieties and bitter disappointments, the furious protests at the way the world goes that may rise as we watch the news, the bafflement about how prayer works, all the restlessness of mind and spirit that gathers around the claim that God is in charge. Here, then, is a picture of a world made by God to be both glorious and unpredictable, and a divine response to the world that is always to do with transformation, the unstoppable pressure of God's work towards a future. It is a pressure at work even – or especially – in the places where we see it least at first sight, where the cry of protest is strongest.

Strange Design

Philip Crowe deploys all his skill and experience as a communicator to put before us a new model of God's rule that makes it always the steady impulse of God, wounded but not defeated, towards the future that is God's Kingdom. This is a clear, vivid and often moving book that repays many readings. I hope it will renew its readers in their trust in God's purpose and God's reign.

Bishop Rowan Williams
August 1999

Preface

Brother Cadfael once remarked that a man who loses his last home may very well revert to his first. The Church in Wales was my first home. I was born in Wrexham, and sang in the parish church choir, where my father was for many years one of the four churchwardens. I am deeply grateful to Archbishop Alwyn, to Bishop Barry Morgan and to the clergy and people of the Church in Wales for welcoming me home so graciously, and for giving me the great privilege of working with men and women in their preparation for various forms of ministry through the St Asaph and Bangor Ministerial Training Scheme. This book is a small token of my gratitude, and in particular for the ministry of Alwyn Rice Jones, Bishop of St Asaph (1982–99) and Archbishop of Wales (1991–9).

Philip Crowe, 1999

Introduction

There is a remarkable irony which sums up human achievement over the course of two millennia. It is that the world's most prestigious prizes for human achievement in physics, chemistry, medicine, literature and, strangest of all, peace, have been funded from profits made from armaments.

Strongly pacifist in his views, Alfred Bernhard Nobel was trained as a chemist. He invented dynamite, gelignite and ballistite, which was later developed into cordite gunpowder. He died in 1896, and left provision in his will for the establishment of the Nobel prizes. In the year of his death, dynamite was used by Irish terrorists to cause several explosions in England.

When David Trimble and John Hume received the peace prize in 1998 for their work in the Irish peace process, their financial reward came from riches originally amassed through the invention of the explosives which caused such destruction and suffering in Enniskillen, Londonderry, Belfast and Omagh.

The two millennia which have passed since the birth of Jesus Christ have witnessed quite wonderful advances in human civilization. They have also witnessed horrendous descents into barbarism. 'There are shades of barbarism in twentieth-century Europe,' writes Norman Davies, 'which would once have amazed the most barbarous of barbarians.'[1]

People of faith believe that both human history and the lives of individuals are in the personal care and the ultimate control of God. The understanding of what that care and control means, and the nature of the God who exerts it, varies. For Moslems, God is sovereign and the will of God is absolute. God wills, human beings accept. For Jews, God is sovereign. God wills; and Jews accept, and question, and laugh, or rail, and question again.

For Christians, God is sovereign; but the nature of God is declared in the birth, the character, the life, the death and the resurrection of Jesus Christ. 'God is Christ-like,' declared Michael Ramsey, 'and in him is no un-Christlikeness at all.' It is this which leads Christians to believe that God is a God of love, and that this God of love is in final, personal control of human life and human history.

That is harder to believe today than it has ever been, and for two main reasons. The first, and most obvious, is that this century has witnessed the worst atrocities that have ever been committed in the whole of human history. It is not simply the scale of the destruction and death in the two world wars which is so dreadful, but the determined and reckless cruelty of it all. Never before has there been such an evil attempt to eliminate an entire race in a single Holocaust. Never before have 66,000 people been vaporized in the single, blinding flash of an atomic explosion.

The second reason is that earlier ages found it easier

to believe in God because they knew comparatively little. Belief in God was a necessary counter-balance to the dark forces of ignorance. As science has advanced, our knowledge of the world and our ability to control the forces of nature have progressed beyond the wildest dreams of our ancestors.

There have been two main consequences of these advances and of the accompanying atrocities. One is that large numbers of people have concluded either that God is redundant, or that there was never a God in the first place. How can a loving God have allowed, without noticeable intervention, the cataclysmic events of the twentieth century? Or, why call on God to fill the gaps in our knowledge when we can, or soon will, fill them ourselves?

For some people, therefore, God has been relegated to those diminishing areas of life which we cannot yet understand or explain or control. Not surprisingly, this 'faith' is derided by many scientists and by others as the relic of a bygone era; as a childish desire 'to keep a hold of nurse, for fear you might find something worse'. For other people, who have 'let go', the scientific understanding of life has completely superseded the life of faith. The world of nature, the creative beauty of art, music and literature, and the material world, are sufficient. The idea that there might be a God who is in personal control of life and of death is at once unnecessary and incredible.

The second consequence is that many of those who do hold to belief in God have retreated into more personal understandings of faith. They believe, very deeply, that God is intimately concerned with every detail of their daily life, and that strong belief is somehow adequate to keep at bay the larger and darker questions about the Holocaust. They believe that God is leading them to buy this car rather than that car, but make little attempt to understand why the same God allows death and destruction in multiple crashes on the motorways. They believe that their employment, or even their lack of it, is a direct result of the will of God; but their faith does not engage with the larger political questions which can have such serious effects on employment prospects.

The start of a new millennium is an appropriate time to be asking questions about the world and God. The word 'providence' now seems curiously old-fashioned, a word which belongs to the Victorian era. It was once in such common use that it gained a life of its own; as with the farmer, annoyed by yet another spell of rain, who exclaimed, 'It's that dratted providence again – but there's one above as'll see justice done.'

The original Greek word means literally 'foreknowledge' or 'foresight', but it has come to mean the care God has for all people, and the belief that the whole of human history is under the final and personal control of a God of love. Properly understood, belief in divine providence is comforting, reassuring and disturbing.

This brief exploration will first consider the ways of divine providence in history, nature and personal life, and will then examine the possibility of miracle, the effect of prayer and the fact of suffering. Where it is natural and unforced, there is a focus on one aspect of the life of Christ, moving chronologically from birth to death. Since 'God was in Christ reconciling the world to himself',[2] it is in the life of Christ that we may expect to find some of the clearest examples of the workings of divine providence.

The concluding chapter offers a restrained view on the immediate future, free of millennium predictions and resolutions, and a hopeful look at the day when, in the providence of God, all will be subject to the just and gentle rule of Christ.

I have tried to think hard and honestly about a difficult subject which embraces many different aspects of life and theology, and which is too often reduced to pious over-simplifications; but I am deeply aware of the fact that, in the words of Job, 'These are but the outskirts of God's ways, and how small a whisper do we hear of him!'[3] The title is taken from Charles Wesley's hymn, 'And can it be'. ''Tis mystery all: the immortal dies,/ Who can explore his strange design.' The verse concludes, 'Let angel minds enquire no more'; but I have always believed that the hymn which says, 'Faith believes nor questions how' should read 'Faith believes and questions how.'

Chapter 1

The Accidents of History

It is a strange fact that the three decades between 1914 and 1945, during which Europe was the centre of two world wars, and in the grip of severe economic depression, began and ended with events which were in part accidental.

On 28 June 1914, Archduke Francis Ferdinand was visiting Sarajevo. In the morning, a gang of amateur assassins – fanatical Serb nationalists acting in league with the Black Hand organization – threw a bomb which exploded, not underneath the Archduke's car, but under the one following. In the afternoon of the same day, the Archduke, somewhat recklessly, went for another drive with the Governor of Bosnia. The chauffeur, not sure which way to go, stopped the car. By chance, he stopped exactly opposite one of the gang, who quickly shot twice, once at the Archduke and again at the Governor. He fatally wounded the Archduke and his wife.

When Franz Ferdinand died, his uncle, the Emperor of Austria-Hungary, is said to have been greatly relieved. 'God permits no challenge,' he muttered. 'A Higher Power has re-established the order which I had no longer been able to maintain.' It is not known whether the comment referred to the Archduke's marriage, or to his passion for the wholesale slaughter of animals, in which he took such savage delight. His assassination was the immediate cause of the First World War.

The Second World War finally came to an end with the dropping of atomic bombs on Hiroshima and Nagasaki. Before the bombs were dropped, there had been some negotiations with the Japanese, to which the Prime Minister of Japan, the eighty-year-old Admiral Suzuki, had given a non-committal reply. By an accident of mistranslation, his reply was made to sound contemptuous.

The conclusion was reached that negotiations would not bring an end to the war, and that a speedy end was necessary to save the lives of Allied troops. It was a conclusion to which some of those who had lavished such frantic labour and expense, such knowledge and skill, on the development of the atomic bomb were not entirely averse. The devastation would have been horrendous in any case, but it was made worse by a wind which blew the bomb slightly off course, so that it exploded over a residential district of Hiroshima.

It can be argued that the chances which affected those two events, at the beginning and ending of the two world wars, made little difference. The assassination of the Archduke was merely the fuse. There would have been another. The political situation was so bad that war was virtually inevitable. The slight drifting of the atomic bomb meant that more people died, not that the course of human history was changed. But the element of chance, which led to the First World War, and increased the devastation at the end of the Second, raises questions about the goodness or the foresight, or both, of the God who is supposed to be in final control of everything that happens, including world history.

In the same way, the reality of human evil raises questions about the goodness or the power of God, or both. It still comes as something of a shock to remember that although a case could just be made for the dropping of one atomic bomb on Hiroshima, there was no justification for a second bomb on Nagasaki. The fact that Nagasaki included a large number of devout Christians only compounds the questions. There are many who think – and they may be right – that the second bomb was of a different kind, and was dropped for purposes of comparison; and that it had to be dropped quickly, before the Japanese surrendered.

It is, of course, possible that the war itself, from beginning to end, was neither the will of God nor the will of man, but an event determined by the course of history. There is a view, once more fashionable than it is today, that the course of human history is determined by factors which are beyond the control of even the most powerful of individuals. Lord Hankey, who was Secretary to the Cabinet for twenty years, and was for a brief time in Chamberlain's War Cabinet, remarked in 1943 that whoever had been in power, the military position would have been exactly the same. Wars had their own rules and their own momentum, which no politician – not even Churchill – had the power to change. Whether Chamberlain, Halifax, Eden or Churchill had been Prime Minister, Hankey argued, the military position in 1943 would, within a mile or so, have been the same.

This view, that history follows a course which human beings are powerless to change significantly, is expressed strongly in the writings of Tolstoy, and generally takes one of two forms. One is the view that human destiny is shaped by large, impersonal forces which are greater and more powerful than any individual. We are controlled, not by the personal choices we make, but by the accidents of birth, by culture and society, by history and tradition, by blind chance and by inexorable fate.

Accordingly, to praise or blame people for their actions is meaningless. It implies that people are free to choose between different courses of action, when in fact their actions are determined by factors largely beyond their control.

The second form of this idea is similar, except that it places more emphasis on human weakness. Life is a swiftly moving river, fed from many sources. We cannot resist the central current. The most we can do is tack and trim, try to avoid obstacles, and use the wind as skilfully as we can to make our brief journey as tolerable as possible. We may intend to make our journey in a particular direction. The chances of success are remote. Human power and resources are not adequate to the task.[1]

In one of his novels, *The New Men*, C. P. Snow tells of the development of the atomic bomb and of the anguish of the scientists who worked on it. When news is first brought to Whitehall that the Americans have the bomb, the reaction of a senior civil servant is uncharacteristically awkward, 'almost stuttering, nothing like his usual brisk tone. "There are times, it seems to me," he said, "when events get too big for men."' Then he adds, in the best traditions of the civil service, '"If so, the only course that I can see is to play one's particular game according to the rules."'[2]

In *Corridors of Power*, written ten years later, he has a discussion between some senior scientists who had worked, twenty years before, on the development of the bomb. 'There's no one of your standing,' one scientist says to a distinguished colleague, 'who's ready to take the risks you took twenty years ago.' Snow adds: 'It wasn't that a new generation of scientists hadn't as much conscience, or as much goodwill or even as much courage. Somehow the climate had changed, they were not impelled. Had the world got too big for them? Had events become too big for men? After sitting silent for some time, one of the scientists said, "At any rate one had to go on acting as though it were not true." '[3]

Even if events seem too big for us, even if history is in the grip of forces beyond our control, even when we feel powerless, our instinct is to deny it and to act as if it were not so. That instinct could, of course, be mere delusion, and a vain exaggeration of our own significance. But in fact there are strong objections to this deterministic understanding of the world. It is a theory for which no scientific evidence can be offered. It cannot be tested. Against it, we may set the evidence of history and experience.

History does supply examples of people whose individual choices have made a difference. Lord Hankey may have adopted an extreme Tolstoyan view when he suggested that whoever had been in power, the position in 1943 would have been virtually the same. In marked contrast, his reflections on the First World War suggest that one individual did make a great deal of difference. After listing the great achievements of Britain's wartime leader, Hankey wrote, 'I wish to place on record my conviction that the man who won the war was David Lloyd George.'[4]

Alexander Fleming, finding a culture dish full of mould in his laboratory, chose to investigate it further. His choice was, in a sense, dictated by the scientist he had become, by an innate curiosity disciplined by scientific method. Nonetheless, the choice he faced, to investigate or to throw it away, was a free choice. The consequence of his choice was, of course, the discovery of penicillin.

Sir Thomas More chose to resist Henry VIII at a time when the King ruled supreme. His determination, his integrity, and his conscience had all been formed by his education, his upbringing, and his devotion to Christ and to the Catholic Church. At the time of 'the King's matter', the urgent question of the succession and the divorce, all the King's subjects were faced with a hard choice between loyalty to the Pope or loyalty to the King. All were under intense pressure from tradition, conscience, and the King's will. All had a free choice, whether or not to sign the Act of Supremacy. All collapsed in supine acquiescence except for a few monks, Bishop Fisher of Rochester and Sir Thomas More; and they were executed.

History furnishes clear examples of people whose free choices made a difference, either to the events themselves, or to the way in which we think about those events. When we look back on the course of history, and on the people who have shaped it, our assessments are, ideally, as objective as possible. We try to know what happened and why, to understand motives, to discover what options were available. To know is to understand, but to understand is not necessarily to forgive. To understand is sometimes to praise, sometimes to blame, sometimes to condemn, sometimes to forgive.

We condemn the racist evil of Hitler and the Nazis. We blame those ordinary members of the Nazi party whose indifference to the plight of the Jews made the Holocaust possible. We praise Oscar Schindler, despite all the glaring flaws in his character, because he recognized the plight of the Jews, and did as much as he possibly could to rescue as many as he could.

We understand the motives of those who trafficked in human life during the slave trade, but understanding of their belief that black people were an inferior species, and of their greed, only leads to greater condemnation. We blame those ordinary people in England and America who enjoyed the benefits of the slave trade without giving any serious thought to it. We praise those who recognized evil when they saw it, and worked for the abolition of slavery.

Even if every possible allowance is made for the determinative influences of their culture, religious beliefs and traditions, we still condemn the white minority in South Africa who devised and implemented the policy of apartheid; and we praise Nelson Mandela for his humanity, his magnanimity and his statesmanship.

We are still not quite sure whether to blame or to forgive Pope Pius XII. As Pope during the Second World War, he had power and responsibility. Had he given a strong and determined lead, the Roman Catholic Church in general, and the Vatican in particular, might have done far more to save the Jews from the Holocaust. But we know, from careful study, that Pope Pius was the wrong man in the wrong place at the wrong time. We know that personally and temperamentally, he was not equal to the task. We know too that the options open to him were very few, and that he did everything he thought he could, including a great deal of secret work which resulted in the rescue of a significant number of Jews.

Had he made a great public gesture in support of the Jews, the consequences might have been far-reaching. But he made few strong pronouncements, no powerful gestures, so we do not know what the results would have been. We can only guess. It might have provided the Jews with a respite. More likely, it would have provoked Hitler to even greater fury. In such circumstances, some people condemn him harshly, some understand and forgive, while others praise him for what he managed to do.

If life were determined by forces beyond the control of individuals, if freedom of choice were an illusion, understanding would be everything, while praise or blame or forgiveness would be meaningless. Yet despite the efforts of some philosophers to persuade us that life is determined by forces beyond our control, we persist in ascribing praise and blame, not through force of habit, nor because we are ignorant or perverse, but because history and experience tell us that people chose freely to act as they did, and that if they had chosen to act differently, they could have done so.

It is not often that human beings are faced with choices which affect the lives of countless others. Most of us will not even merit a footnote in history, let alone attract the praise or blame of future generations. Freedom is normally circumscribed. Available options may be few. The use we make of those options is determined by the people we are, which in turn is shaped by the whole succession of smaller choices which we have made throughout our lives.

Whether small or great, history shows that choices are real. So too does human experience. When we decide to go on holiday here rather than there, to accept this job rather than that, to marry this person, our freedom is not absolute, but it is real. Our choices are limited, but they are genuine. We do not feel, nor do we act, as if our choices are determined by vast historical forces. Our experience tells us that, even with all the limits prescribed by culture, upbringing, tradition, knowledge, time, ability and resources, we still enjoy a measure of freedom, and our choices are real.

Some of the pictures used to describe the relationship between God and the world appear to deny this freedom. Pictures are always limited, and pressed to extremes, they invariably dissolve into absurdity.

God is sometimes described as a dramatist or an author; the supreme playwright creating great works of historical drama. A dramatist invents the characters, devises the plot, and writes the lines; so that all that is left for the players is to think and work themselves into their parts, learn their lines, and act brilliantly. Actors present the illusion of freedom, but none of the reality. Writers are in complete control of their characters. Nabokov once remarked that 'My characters are galley slaves. I am the man on the deck with a whip.' The picture of God as the greatest dramatist or writer of them all breaks down at first glance.

How about God as the supreme chess player? The

picture does give some freedom to anyone who dares accept the challenge of a game, but not much. For who could win against such a formidable opponent?

The one picture which does not break down as soon as you look at it is that of God as the great carpet designer. Fabulously expensive Turkish carpets are made with silk thread, and consist of thousands of knots to the square inch. Most are made by people who take the loom home, and work to a traditional design which is provided for them. But some are designed by a master designer, working in co-operation with the weavers.

The frame is suspended vertically, from floor to ceiling, while the weavers sit on one side, the designer on the other. The pattern is on the designer's side; but the weavers know something of the designer's mind. They look at previous examples of his work, they talk with him, and they do what he wants. Slowly, the pattern evolves. The designer has an idea of what he wants to do, but it is not fixed and unchangeable. He hopes and expects that the weavers will co-operate with him, and will listen to his instructions and suggestions; but he does not know in advance what they are going to do. The pattern takes shape in the interaction between the designer and the weavers.

Ideally, the designer and the weavers work together. But the weavers are free, and in any case, they cannot see the pattern; so either deliberately, or through ignorance or accident, they may push their thread through to the designer in the wrong place. The skill of the designer is such that he is able to take the thread and weave it into the perfect and beautiful pattern which he is creating, until the whole work is complete.

This picture of God as the great carpet designer is not a perfect picture by any means; but at least it does not collapse as soon as it is examined. It allows for genuine human freedom. It avoids the suggestion that God has a perfect plan, made in advance, to which every human being must ultimately submit. The creation of a pattern, which human beings only see when they get to the other side, depends on the interaction between the weavers and the designer, and ultimately on the knowledge and the skill of the designer.[5]

Occasionally, looking back on some particular event or on a sweep of history, it is possible to trace a pattern. Often it is obscure. It is like trying to work out from the reverse of part of a carpet what the whole design is like. But some events are so revealing of the ways of God that they cast light on all the rest.

The story of Joseph in the book of Genesis is such a story. Joseph must have been an unbearable child – daddy's favourite, a dreamer, with no tact. The accounts of his dreams infuriated his older brothers, and it is hardly surprising that they decided to do away with him. Nonetheless, selling him into slavery and telling his father that he was dead was an act of great cruelty.

Joseph's life is then all snakes and ladders. No sooner has he begun to make progress than he falls back again. There is a reminder, in the midst of this catastrophe, that all is not lost. One of the older translations quaintly says that 'The Lord was with Joseph, and he was a lucky fellow.' Eventually, after years of hardship and misery, he interprets Pharaoh's dream, and is given supreme power in Egypt.

The account of his brothers coming to buy corn from

him during the years of famine is one of the most vivid and moving in the whole long history of Israel. The fact that Joseph plays cat and mouse with them does him little credit, but eventually he cannot bear it any longer himself. He makes himself known to his amazed and alarmed brothers.

'So Joseph said to his brothers, "Come near, I pray you". And they came near. And he said, "I am your brother, Joseph, whom you sold into Egypt. And now, do not be distressed or angry with yourselves, because you sold me here; for God sent me before you to preserve life."'[6] His brothers are alarmed and incredulous.

Joseph repeats himself more strongly: 'God sent me before you, to preserve for you a remnant on earth'; and again, even more strongly, and not entirely accurately: 'So it was not you who sent me here, but God'. It was in fact his brothers who had caused him to be in Egypt; but the skill of the designer is such that he is able to take this act of evil and work it so effectively into the pattern, that Joseph can say, 'It was not you who did this, but God.'

At the end of the book, the dreams all come true. Joseph's brothers kneel before him, like the sheaves of corn, and say, 'We are your servants.' Joseph then says the crucial words: 'As for you, you meant evil against me; but God meant it for good, to bring it about that many people should be kept alive, as they are this day.'[7]

His brothers had made a free choice, and it was an act of evil. Not by any stretch of the imagination could it be described as the will of God. But God took that act of evil, and several others which afflicted Joseph, and turned them into good. If his brothers had killed him, the story would not now be told. God would have had to find other ways to preserve the people from famine. This story is told because it offers a glimpse into the ways of God, and sheds light on the rest of human history.

Generally, the pattern is far more obscure and difficult to discern; but faith believes that the great designer is constantly at work, in everything that happens. Acts of great courage and goodness may enliven the pattern, the darkest acts of human evil may change it, making sombre contrasts, but the designer can still achieve something creative and beautiful, weaving a pattern out of acts of co-operation and obedience, as well as out of mistakes, accidents and deliberate evil.

The course of human history is shaped sometimes by the happy conjunction of events, leading to remarkable consequences. Sometimes the forces that determine the course of history seem accidental. Often, it is a combination of circumstances and accidents which is decisive. Sometimes it is deliberate human choice which shapes the destiny of peoples and nations.

The man of the millennium, voted by a poll conducted in late 1998 by the *Today* programme, was William Shakespeare. In 1942, Professor Trevelyan anticipated this result, when he described him as 'the greatest of mankind'. But he points out that Shakespeare had his share of luck, and that without it we might never have heard of him. He writes:

To remote posterity the memorable fact about Elizabethan England will be that it produced the plays of Shakespeare. His work would never have been

produced in any other period than these late Elizabethan and early Jacobean times in which it was his
luck to live. He could not have written as he did, if the
men and women among whom his days were passed
had been other than they were, in habits of thought,
life and speech, or if the London theatres in the years
just after the Armada had not reached a certain stage
of development, ready to his shaping hand.[8]

The fact that individuals, society and history provided
him with abundant raw material; that a new style of
drama and the development of the theatre offered him
greater scope than ever before; that playwrights and
actors were, from the middle of the Elizabethan age,
treated with respect, and that the theatre offered a way
to wealth and honour; all this extraordinary conjunction
of circumstances did not mean that Shakespeare was
bound to write plays. It gave him great opportunity,
which, by his free choice, he took. So on the one hand,
Trevelyan can describe him as 'the greatest of them all',
while on the other hand he says that 'It is to the Elizabethan theatre that we owe Shakespeare and all that he
created. For that, let praise be given to the theatre, and
to the Elizabethans.'[9] And to God?

Sometimes, the intentions of individuals and nations,
and the choices made to implement those intentions, are
thwarted by occurrences over which human beings have
no control at all, and particularly by the weather.

On 15 July 1588 the Spanish Armada came within
reach of the Lizard. It was a magnificent and awe-
inspiring sight: 130 ships, including forty men of war,
sailed slowly up the English Channel in an arrow forma-

tion which covered several miles. By the afternoon of 17 July, the Spanish fleet was anchored off Calais, and the Spanish Commander sought to make contact with troops in the Netherlands, waiting for transport to carry them across the Channel. King Philip II of Spain, an austere and deeply religious man, waited in his gloomy study outside Madrid, fasting and praying.

On the night of 28 July, the English eastern and western fleets came together, and Admiral Howard attacked the Armada. At midnight, he sent in eight fire-ships. The Spanish fleet, desperate to escape the fires, panicked, and when dawn broke, the ships were scattered along the French coast. For eight hours after that, one of the most decisive battles in world history was fought, with neither side gaining the upper hand.

At around three in the afternoon, a wind blew hard from the north-west, driving the Spanish ships towards the treacherous banks of the Flemish coast. Several ships sank or were driven ashore; but then the wind backed to the south-west, and what remained of the Spanish fleet was able to regain deep water. The Spanish commander decided to run for safety through the North Sea and around the coast of Scotland; but the wind which had saved them from the French coast now blew in gale force, and drove the ships through mountainous seas. Ship after ship went down. Many were driven onto the rocks of the northern coasts, and the survivors were massacred.

Less than half of the ships and a third of the men returned safely to Spain. In London, there was a great victory procession and a thanksgiving service in St Paul's, while the wreckage of the Armada lay scattered around the coasts.

It is possible that the English fleet would have won the battle anyway, though that is not certain. But the wind which first blew the Spaniards on to the French coast, and then changed direction and turned into a great and destructive gale, was decisive. Professor Norman Davies comments sardonically that 'God, like King Philip, did not smile on Spain.'[10]

The consequences of that providential victory were far reaching. The fact that it was a victory at sea, and a victory which the English did not abuse, 'proved fundamental to the future development of English-speaking lands, and impressed a special character on England'.[11] If the English had followed up their victory with military conquests in Spain, or had taken over and ruled Spanish colonies in the New World, then the course of human history might have been quite different. England would have developed into a more military society. The United States, Australia and Canada might not have come into being as we now know them.

In fact, the great sea victory left England free of the burden of conquest and rule. It promoted freedom; and it encouraged the Elizabethan spirit of adventure, initiative and self-reliance. Did the course of human history turn upon a freak change in the direction of the wind? Or upon the providential action of God in causing the gales?

Sometimes, it is a combination of human choice and accident which is determinative. In 1910, an international conference was held in Edinburgh. The missionary movement had been making great advances, and in preparation for the Conference, a sober estimate was made of the work which still needed to be done to carry out 'the evangelization of the world in this generation'. There were many who thought that, in the providence of God, this might be possible.

Four years later, the First World War began, and the hopes of Edinburgh were dashed. In October 1918, as 'the War to end all wars' was drawing to its close, William Temple, then Bishop of Manchester, wrote:

Nothing is so likely to damage the peace of the world as the inclusion in the settlement of any terms which seem to any of the peoples involved a humiliation or an outrage. What we want is a peace of which German citizens of AD 1950 or 2000 will be prepared to say, 'That was a settlement dictated by no self-interest in any quarter, but by justice alone.'[12]

In fact, of course, the Treaty of Versailles was a humiliation and an outrage. The settlement was condemned in 1919 by J. M. Keynes as morally wrong and economically catastrophic. It created resentment in Germany, and a political vacuum which Hitler and the Nazis exploited to the full.

Looking back on the period between the wars, it is hard to understand why Churchill was a lone voice, and why Hitler was not resisted strenuously from the very beginning. But even to use the phrase 'between the wars' is to take advantage of hindsight. Hitler's aggression can now be seen for what it was. At the time, it was open to differing interpretations.

By the 1930s, there was widespread recognition that the Treaty of Versailles was unjust, and that the terms of the peace settlement could not endure. In 1932,

Temple, by then Archbishop of York, was adding his weighty voice to growing unease about the Treaty, in a sermon which was strongly critical of the guilt clause which had been included in the Settlement. 'In the Treaty of Versailles,' he wrote in 1933, 'the victorious nations imposed upon the chief vanquished nation an assertion that this nation was the only real culprit. It was disastrous, because it was bound to create in Germany a festering sore of resentment – as has in fact occurred.'[13]

Was it just coincidence that Harold Nicholson's famous memoir, *Peacemaking*, was published in 1933, the year when Hitler came to power; or that Lloyd George's book, *The Truth about the Peace Treaties*, was published in 1938, the year of the Munich Agreement? Both books helped to shape the growing conviction that Hitler and the German people were redressing legitimate grievances, and righting wrongs inflicted on them by the Treaty.

In 1939, when reality was inescapable, it became clear that a new British Prime Minister would be needed. All through the 1930s, the standard remark about Winston Churchill was 'Brilliant, of course, but no judgement'; he was seen as the classic example of a man with a brilliant future behind him. Lloyd George compared him to a chauffeur 'who apparently is perfectly sane and drives with great skill for months, and then suddenly takes you over the precipice'.

It is well known that the majority of Churchill's own party were opposed to his appointment, and that the King did not want to send for him. The obvious choice was thought to be Lord Halifax, and he would almost certainly have been appointed, but for the providential chance that he was a member of the House of Lords. So it was Winston Churchill who found himself summoned to Buckingham Palace. He wrote later:

His Majesty received me most graciously, and bade me sit down. He looked at me searchingly and quizzically for some moments, and then said, 'I suppose you don't know why I have sent for you.' Adopting his mood, I replied, 'Sir, I simply couldn't imagine why.' He laughed and said, 'I want to ask you to form a government.' I said I would certainly do so. At last, I had the authority to give directions over the whole scene. I felt as if I were walking with destiny, and that all my past life had been but a preparation for this hour and for this trial.[14]

Churchill's own description of that experience, as 'walking with destiny', is a little vague. Sir Robert Menzies, the Prime Minister of Australia, was more explicit. During Churchill's funeral, as the procession moved slowly from St Paul's to the Thames, Menzies suggested that in that critical year, God had as much to do with Churchill's appointment as the King. He said:

What was at stake was not some theory of government, but the whole and personal freedom of men and women and children. The battle for them was a battle against great odds. That battle had to be won, not only in the air and on the sea and in the field, but in the hearts and minds of ordinary people. It was then that Winston Churchill was called by Almighty God, as our faith makes us believe.[15]

It is only faith which makes it possible to discern the hand of God in the appointment of Winston Churchill, or in the circumstances which gave rise to the plays of Shakespeare. It is scarcely possible to trace any pattern in the terms of the Treaty of Versailles, or in the rise of Hitler and the Nazis, which led to the Second World War and the Holocaust. What God did with those events is hidden from us. The pattern is on God's side, and is not visible to us. The belief that 'you meant it for evil, but God meant it for good' is an act of faith.

Historical events, without exception, can be understood in straightforward human terms without any reference to God, as the consequences of human action; or as the consequence of a combination of human action and natural forces. Faith in God does not change the events themselves, only the way in which those events are perceived.

Over thirty years ago, Max Warren, one of the great Christian visionaries of the twentieth century, was asked about the future of the Christian gospel in China. It was suggested to him that when the Communists came to power, the sudden destruction of so much devoted missionary work must have led him to question the belief that God is in control of human history. He replied:

> The Chinese people have always inclined to respond to a question or a challenge by saying both/and, never yes or no. The Communists demand that they choose. The Christian gospel also requires decision. When Communism begins to lose its way, and Chinese society becomes more open, we may find that the

period of Communist rule has been a most effective preparation for the gospel.

It is unlikely that Mao Tse Tung had any intention of preparing the Chinese people to respond to the gospel of Christ, but to the eye of faith, even the most unlikely events are open to strange possibilities.

Only a few of those who witnessed the events in Galilee and Jerusalem 2,000 years ago recognized in them the presence of God. Most people knew nothing of them, or dismissed them as fairly minor occurrences in an obscure province of the Empire. Anatole France tells a story of Pontius Pilate meeting, in old age, with a friend from his days in Judea. 'Do you remember the Jewish man, Jesus,' the friend asks, 'who was executed for some crime or other?' Pilate pauses for a moment before replying, 'Jesus? Jesus the Jew? No, I don't remember him.'[16]

Flavius Josephus, a Jewish historian of the first century who wrote extensively on Jewish and Roman history, includes only the briefest mention of Jesus of Nazareth. But his histories, like the New Testament, are thick with the consequences of the *Pax Romanum*, and the freedom to travel, the roads and the language which were results of that Roman peace.

The great question, why was Jesus born at that particular time, in that particular place, hinges upon looking at the Jewish dispersion and the Roman Empire with the eyes of faith. 'When the time had fully come,' writes St Paul, 'God sent forth his Son.'[17] The age of prophecy had long since passed, messianic expectation was confused and uncertain, the Jewish people were derided and powerless, Judea was a despised outpost of a great

Empire. Neither the time nor the place looked particularly propitious for the birth of the Messiah.

With hindsight, it is possible to recognize that it was exactly the right time. In 600 BC, Nebuchadnezzar destroyed Palestine and took the Jews away into exile. From that time onwards, the process was repeated many times, with the result that all around the Middle East there were Jewish communities that knew the law, were waiting for the Messiah and were attracting God-fearers. They served as stepping-stones for the gospel.

From 336 to 323 BC Alexander the Great ruled an empire which embraced most of the Mediterranean world. The colonies he established were deliberately mixed and, as Professor Moule comments, 'this must have been a new and powerful factor in blending the dialects: probably the most powerful, in fact, until the advent of printing'.[18] The language which emerged, common Greek, was the language in which the New Testament was later written.

The subsequent rise of Roman power completed the preparation. Palestine may have been on the fringes of the Empire, but it was part of one world, governed by the Emperor and preserving, within its borders, the Roman peace. There was one language used for commerce throughout the Empire. There were roads, along which it was possible and generally safe to travel. Within a relatively short time, the gospel was carried to every part of the Empire, people became Christians and churches were established.

With the possible exception of the end of the nineteenth century, when similar conditions existed in the Western world, it is not easy to think of a period of time so favourable to the quiet beginnings and the easy spread of a new and strange belief. Today, of course, the advent of the Messiah would be announced on the Internet, perhaps with a website called 'www.messiah. co.Israel'; and his coming would probably be a one-day wonder, lost in the clamour of the Web, hailed and as swiftly forgotten in the transient concerns of the media.

Some suggestions for reflection

As for you, you meant evil against me; but God meant it for good, to bring it about that many people should be kept alive, as they are this day. (Genesis 50:20)

Is it right to describe any of the great events of history, the fire of London, for instance, or the Black Death or the Second World War, as being 'neither the will of God nor the will of man'?

Is the picture of the carpet designer valid and helpful; and can you think of better pictures?

Which phrase provides the most adequate description of Churchill's appointment, 'walking with destiny' or 'called by Almighty God'?

Chapter 2

Why a Bee Dances

It happened over thirty years ago, but I can still see it clearly. I was driving along a straight road, and another car was coming towards me. When the car was about thirty metres away, a tiny animal started to cross the road from my side. The timing was perfect and tragic. The animal went straight under the centre of the front off-side wheel and was squashed completely flat.

I was young, a Christian, and believed that God was in control of everything, that not even a sparrow 'will fall to the ground without your Father's will'.[1] I thumped the driving wheel of my car and shouted out 'Why?'

Professor Richard Dawkins tells us that the question 'Why?' is one that we cannot and should not ask. It is meaningless. Life just is:

In a universe of blind physical forces and genetic replication, some people are going to get hurt, other people are going to get lucky, and you won't find any rhyme or reason in it, or any justice. The universe we observe has precisely the properties we should expect if there is, at bottom, no design, no purpose, no evil and no good, nothing but blind, pitiless indifference.[2]

Why a Bee Dances

It is possible and right, says Dawkins, to ask why a bee dances, or why seal colonies have such a large number of useless males, or why downy willows send out such vast quantities of seed. A scientific answer can be given. But the fact that human beings have purpose on the brain, that we have to ask 'Why?' of everything, does not always make the question appropriate nor the answers meaningful. To ask why a young man is struck down by a paralysing disease, or why this person lives to be ninety-six and that person lives to be only thirty-six, or why this tiny animal has to run precisely into the path of that wheel, is simply not appropriate. No answer can be given except, that's the way life is.

Dawkins is a distinguished scientist reacting to a jibe which scientists frequently have to suffer. Scientists, it is said, are good at the 'How?' questions but useless at the 'Why?' questions. They are good tin-openers, but they have no idea of what to do with the contents.

It is hardly surprising that scientists get tired of such comments. A great many scientists are deeply concerned, as human beings, about the implications and the human consequences of their discoveries; often more concerned than the rest of us, because they know more. They are also inclined to resent the assumption which lies behind the question, that because scientists are supposedly not qualified to answer the 'Why?' questions, there are other disciplines which are – an assumption which Professor Dawkins rightly describes as 'quite illogical'.

Until 1859, both the 'How?' and the 'Why?' questions received the same answer. It was widely believed that the whole of creation and all of life owed its origin to the purpose and will of a good and loving creator

God. Of course, 1859 was the date of the publication of Darwin's *Origin of Species*. From the moment the book was published, there were two schools of thought, one holding that Darwin's views were consistent with religion, the other holding equally firmly that they were not.

The Duke of Argyll visited Darwin and talked with him about orchids. Argyll held that such beauty and delicacy must be the expression of a good and purposeful mind. Darwin looked at him 'very hard' before replying and said, 'Well, that often comes over me with overwhelming force; but at other times' – and he shook his head vaguely – 'it just seems to go away.' But Darwin was being polite. To a friend he complained that the Duke, 'who knows my orchid book so well, might have learned a lesson of caution from it'. His Grace's talk of beauty for beauty's sake showed that, 'like any politician, he was all mouth and no ears'. Darwin himself found that the more he knew of scientific development, the less he believed in God.[3]

It is widely believed that the Christian Church has still not really come to terms with evolution, and holds to the story in Genesis that the world was created by God in six days. There are, it is true, a few who hold that evolution is contrary to the Bible, but they are a tiny minority.

In 1884, just twenty-five years after Darwin's great work had been published, Frederick Temple delivered the Bampton Lectures on *The Relations between Religion and Science*. His lectures accept that the theory of evolution is right. Twelve years later, Temple was appointed Archbishop of Canterbury. By then, evolution was at least permissible and respectable amongst all educated Christians.

When Darwin died, in 1882, his close friend and colleague, Thomas Huxley, thought about asking for him to be buried in Westminster Abbey, but decided against it, thinking that the request would be refused. He was told, by Canon Farrar, that 'we clergy are not all so bigoted as you suppose'; and Darwin was buried with Christian rites in the Abbey.[4]

By now, our understanding of evolution has reached the point where Professor Dawkins suggests that life and all its developments can be explained in terms of the transmission of DNA and the dominance of the selfish gene. If we ask why a bee dances, or why a seal colony includes so many useless males, or why the downy willow throws out so many seeds, the answer is to be found in natural selection and the transmission of DNA.

Natural selection is not random. It does not happen by chance. Mutation is random. Natural selection happens on purpose, over amazingly long periods of time. The purpose is survival, and survival demands the transmission of DNA, the core of life itself, to another generation. The species which survive are those which adapt most effectively to the world around them.

I am not a biologist, and am not qualified to pronounce on the scientific case for evolution; but I find the writings of Professor Dawkins fascinating and convincing. What I do not understand is why he uses his scientific conclusions to dismiss altogether the idea of God. To explain how the world works, or why certain species develop as they do, does not prove that there is no God. Even the most complete scientific account of the natural world does not necessarily exhaust the whole meaning of it.

Natural selection, and the transmission of DNA, may explain a great deal about the natural world, and about the behaviour of humans, but it does not explain everything. Human beings do not dance solely to the tune of DNA. We may act selfishly, in our determination not merely to survive but to flourish. We are also capable of self-sacrifice to the point of death. We may act with great cruelty, but we sometimes behave with nobility. We may preserve our own belongings at whatever cost, but we can also be generous. We are capable of extraordinary cruelty and of great goodness. We can be creative in artistic ways which are, strictly speaking, quite useless.

It is quite legitimate for Dawkins to say of God, with Laplace, 'I have no need of that hypothesis'; but he seems to go beyond the evidence of even his own extensive research and his persuasive conclusions when he maintains, somewhat dogmatically, that there is no God, and that natural selection is all there is. The most that he can, or should, say is, 'I can offer a scientific explanation of how and why life has reached this particular point in its development, and for me, this explanation is sufficient.' He can argue that a scientific understanding of evolution cannot easily be reconciled with the traditional understanding of a God of love, but still he cannot prove, scientifically, that there is no God.

Others may choose to look at the scientific evidence and the conclusions drawn from it with the eyes of faith. It is not necessary, as Bishop Montefiore does, to question evolution, or to suggest that its explanations are incomplete, in a desperate attempt to make some space for God. There are scientific understandings of the world which are wholly inconsistent with belief in God. Evolution, it seems to me, is not one of them. It is quite possible to believe in natural selection and in God. Natural selection tells us a great deal about how the natural world functions; faith tells that it is God who has created and who sustains the world through the long processes of evolution.

The experience of a Christian struggling to come to terms with a different branch of science may offer a useful parallel. Dr John Baillie was a distinguished Scottish professor of theology. He was born into a Christian family, and from earliest childhood, he was brought up with a sense of the presence of God. When he was a student in the earlier years of this century, there were quite a few scientists who believed that the universe is a gigantic mechanism.

The most extreme form of this belief was put famously by Pierre Simon de Laplace, who argued that the laws of motion dictated the behaviour of even the smallest atom in the most minute detail. Give me a large enough calculator, Laplace contended, and information about the laws of motion and the exact state of the universe at a given moment, and, in theory at least, it would be possible to predict with complete certainty and accuracy the exact state of the world at any given moment in the future.

Such a mechanistic universe clearly excludes the possibility of human freedom. 'A machine can have no free will,' writes Professor Paul Davies; 'its future is rigidly determined from the beginning of time. Indeed time ceases to have much physical significance in this picture, for the future is already contained in the present. Time merely turns the pages of a cosmic history book that is already written.'[5]

It might conceivably be allowed that God is the original inventor of such a machine, but having set life in motion, God is a spectator. There could be no divine control over the world. What would be, would be. There could be no chance, no accident, no divine intervention, no providence.

Even though he felt himself confined in a strait-jacket of scientific thought, John Baillie still found himself 'quite unable to escape from the sense of God's presence with me in mercy and judgement ... but I could not conceive how the two could possibly be harmoniously entertained within a single total outlook, and I suffered much from the resulting intellectual schism'.[6]

In 1927, two things occurred which rescued him from this intellectual distress. One was a series of lectures – the Gifford lectures, delivered in Edinburgh University by Eddington on *The Nature of the Physical World*. The other was the enunciation, by Heisenberg, of the principle of indeterminacy. Together they demonstrated that Laplace's calculator simply would not work. The universe is not like that.

Eddington and Heisenberg argued that everything we can measure is subject to random fluctuations. If Laplace had been able to record the exact position of every atom in the universe at a precise moment, he could not have calculated the velocity of a single one. There is, in the natural world, an element of genuine unpredictability.

Baillie used the picture of a container, with a partition

in the middle. In one end, there is white sand, in the other, red. The partition is removed, and the container shaken. The result is that 'we can count on soon obtaining a fairly equal distribution, it being highly unlikely that the original clear division will ever again be restored after no matter how many further shakings'.[7]

The movement of each particular grain of sand – how far or how fast it will go – cannot be predicted or controlled. The grains move randomly, but the end result will almost invariably be the same. However many times the experiment is repeated, the result can be predicted with a high degree of probability. The illustration indicates clearly that despite Eddington's lectures and Heisenberg's uncertainty principle, the new physics still retains an element of determinism. The results of random movement can be predicted.

The element of randomness, and consequently of freedom, was, however, enough for John Baillie. The new physics released him from the strait-jacket of absolute determinism. He adds:

> Needless to say, this new scientific conception of the physical universe offers no more positive evidence of the presence of God in the world or of his providential ordering of it than did the older one. What it does do is leave more room for these things, if they can be established on other grounds.[8]

Baillie died in 1960, three years before Edward Lorenz offered the first tentative hints of what later became known as chaos theory. Lorenz's famous paper, delivered in 1979, bore the title, 'Does the flap of a butterfly's wings in Brazil set off a tornado in Texas?' Originally Lorenz spoke of a seagull's wings, but a butterfly was more dramatic.

Chaos theory, if I understand it rightly, works like this. Two movements are begun simultaneously. The force applied to one movement is consistent, so the movement also is consistent and predictable. The other movement is subject to slight variations in force. As a result, the variations in its movement may grow so fast that they become chaotic and completely unpredictable.

It is not a perfect picture, but the different consequences of determinist and chaotic views of the universe are put like this by Professor Robert May. He suggests:

> Imagine a road lined with telegraph poles in a perspective drawing. Given two or three poles, you can easily draw in the rest for yourself. But nature often draws itself differently. Imagine a river running alongside the road. The water has flat bits and bumpy bits. However many I draw in for you, there is no way for you to tell where the next flat or bumpy bit is going to be.[9]

Evidently (it is at least evident to some physicists and mathematicians) the universe is made up of chaotic and non-chaotic systems, and its future is genuinely unpredictable. It is not a book already written, whose pages need only to be turned. 'The final chapter of the great cosmic book has yet to be written.'[10]

Had he lived to learn this, John Baillie would have realised that the strait-jacket of determinism does not exist. Classical physics, of the kind advocated by

Laplace, imposed such restrictions on the understanding of divine providence as to make it virtually meaningless. The new science does at least allow for the possibility that there may be both human freedom and divine action in this one world, and that science and religion may be complementary, rather than contradictory.

Some scientists, like a great many other people, view the universe with the eyes of science and with the eyes of faith, and these are different and complementary ways of looking at the same body of evidence. The principle of complementarity was first introduced into physics by Niels Bohr, who was one of the great pioneers in atomic science. Light consists of waves and particles, and to understand how it can consist of both at the same time, it is necessary to give different accounts of the same phenomena. The scientific and the religious approaches to the universe are not different approaches to two different worlds, but complementary approaches to the same world.

A doctor may give as complete a medical account of a disease as it is possible to give. He is an observer, studying it in minute detail. But his approach to the same disease is likely to take on new dimensions if his wife is diagnosed as a sufferer.

A person who is unable to read could dismiss printing as a meaningless series of ink blobs on a piece of paper. From one point of view, he would be entirely right. There is only ink on the paper. But the meaning of the writing is not something left over when the literal explanations are exhausted. The meaning can only be found by a different approach to exactly the same information.

The classic example of this is the rainbow. From a

scientific point of view it can easily be explained. In the days of Noah, no such explanations were available; but rainbows must have appeared in the sky before the flood. What happened after the flood was that a familiar sight was invested with new meaning. It was used as a sign of God's promise, that never again would the inhabited world be devastated by such a great flood. Today a scientist can look at a rainbow and see light. A person of faith may look at the same rainbow, and see the reminder of a promise.

Christians sometimes think and argue as if the world of science and the world of faith were entirely separate. The effect is to turn God into a ghost who mysteriously haunts old houses after many scientists claimed to have finished God off. But God is either there, in the natural world and in the scientific accounts of it, or God does not exist at all.

Religious convictions about the way in which God works in the world have, for many centuries, been fed by unscientific views of the universe. Partly, of course, this is because faith has developed over centuries, long before evolution or the new physics were discovered. Partly it is for the less honourable reason that people of faith sometimes take from science what suits them, and forget the rest.

David Attenborough was once asked whether being so close to the natural world had affected his attitude to religion and to God. His answer was distinctly non-committal:

People do sometimes say, when you see extraordinary natural beauty, say a humming bird, or a bird of paradise, don't you feel that is proof of the Almighty. But you must not just think of humming birds. You've also got to think of a parasitic worm boring into the eye of a small child living on the banks of an African river, and presumably that worm too is created by the Almighty; so I don't think that the complexity of the natural world or its beauty or its savagery is necessarily anything to do with religious conviction about a deity.[11]

Dawkins argues that cheetahs are superbly designed to kill antelopes, and that antelopes, equally impressively, are designed to survive, and to cause starvation among cheetahs. This does not cause him to wonder at the skill of the great designer. On the contrary, he suggests that a God who created the tiger and the lamb, the cheetah and the gazelle, might be a sadist taking special delight in blood-sports.

If we are to believe in God and believe in evolution, then our faith must take account of both the glory and the savagery of creation. Otherwise it would be better not to believe at all, to accept that nature is blind, pitiless and indifferent, concerned solely with survival, and that there is no God.

Christians once derived a good deal of their belief in divine providence from the natural world. From Psalm 19, 'The heavens declare the glory of God and the firmament shows his handiwork', to the Sermon on the Mount, 'Consider the lilies of the field', nature was held to reinforce the view that the world is in the loving care of a God who is good.

A hymn like 'The spacious firmament on high, with

all the blue ethereal sky, and spangled heavens a shining frame, their great original proclaim', which was written by Joseph Addison in the eighteenth century, has not yet been overtaken by the new physics. 'All things bright and beautiful', written by Mrs Alexander, who was born just nine years after Charles Darwin, is far more problematical. 'He made their glowing colours, he made their tiny wings' may be true, but it is a sentimental view of nature and is so partial as to be seriously misleading. 'All things blind and pitiless, the Lord God made them all'?

Alfred Tennyson was born in the same year as Darwin. They were at Cambridge together and both belonged to a radical, free-thinking group called the Apostles. Unlike Mrs Alexander, he recognizes the challenge posed to traditional Christian faith by Darwin.

> Are God and nature then at strife,
>   That nature lends such evil dreams?
>   So careful of the type she seems,
> So careless of the single life;
>
> That I, considering everywhere
>   Her secret meaning in her deeds,
>   And finding that of fifty seeds
> She often brings but one to bear,
>
> I falter where I firmly trod,
>   And falling with my weight of cares
>   Upon the world's great altar-stairs
> That slope through darkness up to God,

Who trusted God was love indeed
And love creation's final law –
Though nature, red in tooth and claw
With ravine, shrieked against his creed.[12]

In pre-evolution days, it was recognized that the natural world is not exactly gentle; but this was explained by traditional understandings of the doctrine of the Fall. The belief has been substantially changed in the light of biblical study, but in its traditional form, it was derived from Genesis chapter 3, and confirmed in Christian theology by St Paul in his letter to the Romans.

The Fall was held to be an event which happened near to the beginning of time. Because the first human beings sinned, by wilful disobedience to God's command, sin and evil entered the world and have, ever since, been transmitted from one generation to the next. The natural world has, in consequence, been 'subjected to futility . . . and groans in travail'. God is good, but neither human beings nor the natural world are now as God originally intended.

Evolution now indicates that the doctrine of the Fall is not an adequate or even a possible explanation. The principle of natural selection, and the survival of whatever species adapts best to its environment, has been the guiding principle from the very beginning. The transmission of DNA was the controlling principle long before human beings evolved, and is built into the created order itself. It is no longer possible to credit God with what is good and to blame human beings for what is savage.

St Paul tells us that 'from the beginning of creation,

God's invisible nature has been clearly perceived in the things that have been made'.[13] If our understanding of God is derived, in part at least, from creation, then we have to recognize that God is a God of determined purpose and devastating severity, that life is preserved and developed at great cost, and that God is responsible. There is glory, beauty and balance in nature. There is also ugliness, waste and suffering. The same creator God must be responsible for all of it, or none of it.

If the Christian faith is to have any credibility, then Christians must give an account of the world which does not leave out the uncomfortable facts, which takes seriously the way the world is, and which offers a reasonable and convincing explanation for it. Why is the world like this? What might God's purpose be in such a world?

Professor Dawkins uses a method of reasoning known as 'reverse engineering'. An archaeologist finds a long, rusting, curved, metal blade with a hole near the thicker end. He wonders what it was used for. He tries various ways of attaching a handle to it, and concludes that an upright handle, with the blade at right angles, and a support making use of the hole in the blade, seems to suit it best. He tests it out in a number of different ways, and discovers that it is ideally suited to cutting great swathes of grass with a steady, flowing movement. By asking what it could be used for, he has discovered the true purpose of a scythe.

The universe is a world of beckoning beauty and great danger. If we ask, 'What is it for?' the simplest answer is, 'It exists for the transmission of life.' That may be all. But equally, there may be more to it than that.

Human beings may be intended for greater things than survival and shopping.

The Christian understanding of God is not based on creation alone, but is rooted even more firmly in the long history of the chosen people. There too, as in nature, God's purpose is resolute and demanding. To this day, the Jewish people regard their choice by God as a somewhat mixed blessing. 'Why did he have to choose us? Why not someone else for a change?!'

The story begins with the call of Abraham, who was commanded to sacrifice his only son. It reaches its great climax in the sacrifice of Christ, who pleaded with God to 'let this cup pass from me', while at the same time accepting grievous suffering and death as the will of God.

In between, the Israelites are required to give absolute allegiance to God and to none other. They are required to eliminate their enemies. When they sin, they are punished harshly, sometimes with devastating severity. History confirms what nature suggests.

God is a shepherd, guiding gently, protecting and nurturing, with great care. God is also a consuming fire, making absolute demands and requiring total, though not always unquestioning, obedience.

It is precisely because God is both a consuming fire and our refuge and strength that it is possible for human beings to 'grow into mature humanity, measured by nothing less than the stature of Christ'.[14] The best teachers of the violin are those whose standards are utterly demanding. They are encouraging and appreciative, but it is the awareness of the seemingly impossible standards they set which calls out the best in those who have the inclination and the aptitude to become great violinists.

Human beings are destined for glory. We have the inclination and the aptitude to share in the life of God and to enjoy the glorious liberty of the children of God. Our highest good is to enjoy a personal relationship with God. A personal relationship at the highest level is only possible on two conditions. First, the two people must recognize each other's distinctiveness. They must respect each other's values, and intentions, and desires, and freedom. They must also have each other's best interests at heart. 'The most precious gift marriage gave me,' writes C. S. Lewis, 'was this constant impact of something very close and intimate, yet all the time unmistakably other, resistant – in a word, real.'[15]

A personal relationship with God is possible because God is absolute demand and gentle strength. A relationship with God may require the same conditions as human relationships, but it is not the same. It is not a cosy friendship, or a meeting of equals. God comes to us as absolute and unconditional demand, with the purest, most severe love.

This has two consequences. First, it makes us aware of our freedom. We can choose whether to respond or not. We are free to accept God's love and to begin to love both God and other people, or to neglect and reject it. There can be no genuine, personal relationship of love without that freedom.

Secondly, if we do respond, the love of God requires all that we are. The absolute demand of God is more sacred than life itself. It is stronger even than that most powerful of desires, the urge to remain alive.

If now we 'reverse engineer' the created order, we know that God has created a world of great beauty and extreme danger; a world of determined purpose and of unbounded opportunity. It is a world in which we are free to live at the level of creatures, ruled by appetites, desires, needs and instincts; or we can respond to the absolute demand of God.

The world offers the conditions in which human beings can become the people God means us to be. With divine foresight, God has created a world in which there is freedom and opportunity, danger and demand, beauty and suffering. If we lose ourselves in the love of God, we find our true freedom. We are no longer the prisoners of DNA, or natural selection, or material existence. In acknowledging values which are greater even than life itself, we are free to live, rather than merely exist.

God demands that Abraham kill his only son. It is a cruel, even a barbaric demand. If survival, and the transmission of DNA were all, Abraham could not do it; and every instinct and affection in him cried out against this demand of God. But in response to God's absolute demand, he brings himself, by sheer obedience, to the point where he will kill his son.

From one point of view, this makes him a savage. From another, it makes him genuinely human. He has acknowledged and submitted to values higher than mere survival. He is prepared to lose his life; and in losing it, he finds it. So he is called God's friend. The description is unique in the Bible, and so is the demand. It is there, at the beginning of the story of Israel, to show us starkly the meaning of life.

Jesus too responds to the absolute demand of God by

offering up his own life. Jesus was deeply aware of God, more deeply than any other human being who has ever lived. He knew God as absolute demand and as perfect love.

His teaching sets out the absolute and uncompromising demands of the rule of God. 'You must be perfect, as your Father in heaven is perfect.' 'If your hand offends you, cut it off.' 'Love the Lord your God with all your heart, and with all your soul, and with all your strength and with all your mind; and your neighbour as yourself.' 'Whoever would save his life will lose it; and whoever loses his life for my sake will save it.'[16]

The natural world, with its beauty and its severity, reflects the will and purpose of God, who is, in the words of Dante, 'The Lord of terrible aspect', both a consuming fire and our refuge and strength, 'whose service is perfect freedom', and in whose will is our peace.

Some suggestions for reflection

The world is a place of beckoning beauty and inspiring interest. An African girl, standing on a high rock, looked out over miles and miles of country and up into a clear blue sky. 'I can see the world,' she cried, 'and I can touch the feet of God.'

What response would you make to a scientist who claimed that science has proved that God does not exist?

Why a Bee Dances

'The heavens declare the glory of God' – but what do slugs, and cabbage root fly, and parasitic worms declare about God?

Is it 'reasonable and convincing' to suggest that God has created a world of extreme beauty and great danger in order to provide the conditions in which human beings may grow into maturity?

Chapter 3

Did Jesus Find Me a Parking Space?

David Attenborough became a television presenter quite by chance. In 1952, he was a producer working in the new medium of television in the days when there were just a few producers making programmes about anything they could think of. Together with a friend from London Zoo, he decided to make a series of programmes about animals, to be called *Zoo Quest*.

After the first week, the presenter from London Zoo was taken seriously ill, and as the programmes were live, someone had to take his place. The Director said to David Attenborough, 'You'll have to do it'; and, he added quickly, 'As you're BBC staff, you'll get no fee.' By such a chance, the career of one of the most successful television presenters was launched.

John Arlott, whose rich, plummy voice and brilliant descriptions delighted cricket fans for many years, became a cricket commentator also by chance. It was, he once said,

sheer accident. I was in the Eastern service of the BBC broadcasting to India and Malaysia and South East Asia, and the BBC decided to let India know that they realised an Indian Cricket team was playing in

England. They sent me off to do ten minutes a day on each of the first two matches, intending not to do any more; and they sent me solely for the reason that since I worked in that section I was presumed to know how to pronounce the Indian names. That's the only reason I was sent.[1]

A senior police officer in the West Midlands force went out one day to get his hair cut, and was walking back to his office when he slipped on a piece of fruit and fell so heavily that he ruptured his thigh muscle. Not realising that he had damaged himself so badly, he struggled to his feet and tried to walk, fell again, and ruptured the thigh muscle in his other leg. After some weeks in hospital, he returned to his office, and out of curiosity, asked for the police report of his accident. The message which had reached the police switchboard was that 'an old man has fallen in the subway'. He decided to retire. Six months later, he died.

A man travels to work by train every morning. He gets on the same train, at the same time, and sits at the same table with three friends. One morning he is late, and misses his train by seconds. Near Clapham, there is a crash. The carriage in which he would have been travelling is crushed. His friends, sitting at the table at which he would have sat, are all killed.

My wife and I were once in grave doubt about whether to accept a particular job. My wife said jokingly, as we looked around the town, 'I'm not moving here unless there's a Sainsbury's.' Thirty seconds later, we heard someone calling out to a friend, 'I'll see you in Sainsbury's in five minutes.' Was it chance, or coincidence, or God? Was that rumble in the sky a laugh?

Such life-changing accidents or coincidences or chances are fairly common. And even if the consequences are not especially dramatic, most people experience good luck or bad luck at some point in their lives. For older generations, such experience was a pointer to another world, a hidden world of forces – some good, some evil – which were constantly bearing down upon human life. Many old superstitions, such as throwing salt over the left shoulder into the devil's eye, were intended to placate malevolent powers.

For people of faith, nothing happened by chance. Luck, fortune and chance were the devil's trinity. Everything was intended by God, and was sent to encourage, to punish, to guide or to warn; and this belief survives today in the way we think and speak about chance.

A tile falls off a roof and kills a passer-by. We say that it happened 'by chance'. If he had only been going a little faster, or a little slower, it would have smashed harmlessly on the pavement; and had it done so, the man would have had 'a lucky escape'. In either case, we speak of chance or luck only because a person is involved. If the wind had caught the tile in the night, and the remains had been found on the ground next day, we would think nothing of it.

It is because the tile happened to fall at the precise moment when someone was passing underneath that we speak of chance; though the use of that word can carry different meanings. To describe it as chance may be a way of saying, 'It just happened', and there was no meaning and no intention in it. It was simply an accident. But to speak of chance may imply that there was some intention in the tile falling; and from there it is a short step to wondering if it happened on purpose. Why this particular person, at that precise moment?

Earlier generations would have invested that chance happening with meaning. They might have wondered if the tile had fallen as a punishment, because the person was on the way to commit a crime. They might have feared that the tile was moved, or even inhabited, by an evil spirit which needed propitiating.

It is easy to dismiss such ideas as a primitive response to the universe, a return to the animism of our ancestors. But even this 'primitive' response may point to a deeper truth, that there is some ultimate significance in all reality; that nothing ever happens by chance; that luck, fortune and chance really are the devil's trinity.

'In all things,' writes St Paul, 'God works together for good with those who love him, those who are called according to his purpose.'[2] Leave aside, for the moment, the limitation in the kind of people to whom this applies. The major assertion is that God works for good in everything.

St Paul himself gives instances of this. He was afflicted by a minor but troublesome physical weakness, possibly something wrong with his eyes. Three times he prayed that God would remove it, and nothing happened. The answer he received was, 'My grace is sufficient for you, because my strength is made perfect in weakness.'[3] Paul clearly believed that God could have removed it, but chose not to, for the greater good.

In his frequent journeying, Paul moves around for various reasons. Sometimes he decides where to go because he has a clear strategy in mind, and is concentrating on major centres of communication. He went to Macedonia because he tried to preach in two other places and was prevented 'by the Spirit of Jesus'; and a vision in the night told him where to go next. Later, he decided to go to Rome because he was a Roman citizen, and took advantage of his right of appeal to the Emperor. Whatever the reason for his destination, whatever the means by which he gets there, he is quite sure that God is leading him, and going before him, and that in all things God is working with him for good. That has been, and still is the faith of a great many Christians.

One is in need of a minor operation, and a bed becomes available at precisely the right moment. A Christian charity is in urgent need of money, and a surprise donation for just the right amount arrives anonymously in the post. A person goes to the midweek church prayer meeting, and offers thanks to God for the fact that just as she was driving into town to do the shopping, a parking place became available. A young Christian man meets someone, and their relationship develops. After a good deal of prayer, he proposes to her by saying, 'God has told me that we should get married.' She replies, forcefully, 'Well, he hasn't told me!' But eventually God must have done, because they were married and enjoyed a good partnership for over sixty years.

What are we to make of such occurrences (none of which is invented). The belief that God finds parking places, or organizes the whole of the railway timetable so that a Christian can arrive on time, has become something of a cliché, and it is treated hilariously by Wendy Cope in her 'Strugnell's Christian Songs':

Did Jesus Find Me a Parking Space?

When I went out shopping,
I said a little prayer,
Jesus help me park the car
For you are everywhere.

Jesus in his goodness and grace,
Jesus found me a parking space
In a very convenient place.
Sound the horn and praise him!

His eternal car-park
Is hidden from our eyes.
Trust in him and you will have
A place beyond the skies.

Jesus, in his goodness and grace,
Wants to find you a parking space.
Ask him now to reserve a place.
Sound the horn and praise him![4]

The idea that God intervenes in the world in such small ways for the convenience of certain favoured people can easily be treated as a joke. But there is a serious argument behind the belief that God is concerned with the smallest details of life. It is advanced by Plato:

If a physician, whose office is to cure a body as a whole, were to neglect its small parts while caring only for the greater, will the whole ever prosper in his hands? Nor would it be any better with pilots, or generals or housekeepers. Let us not then think that God, who is the wisest of beings and both willing and able to exercise care, takes no care at all of those things which, being small, are easier to take care of, but attends only to the greater things like some idle good-for-nothing who is tired of his work . . .[5]

Jesus also teaches that God's care extends to details:

For only a penny you can buy two sparrows, yet not one sparrow falls to the ground without your Father's consent. As for you, even the hairs on your head have all been counted.[6]

A keen bridge player, who was also a Christian, once found that his enthusiasm for the game was running away with him; so much so, that when the cards were against him, or his partner made a bad call, he got irritable, and sometimes bad-tempered. He then had a long run of very poor cards, which was so long and so bad that he began to wonder what was happening. It suddenly occurred to him that God was in it, teaching him both perspective and patience. 'If the hairs on my head are all numbered,' he remarked, 'why not also the cards in my hand?'

But does the belief that the hairs on our heads or the cards in our hands are counted necessarily mean that God personally directs us to the best hairdresser or arranges for the cards to be dealt in a particular order? The way in which some Christians talk implies, sometimes even states, that God looks after everything for them, and is in direct personal control of every detail of their lives. The reverse side of this belief implies that God takes a malicious pleasure in intervening in our lives simply in order to frustrate our intentions. 'If you want to make God laugh,' said Woody Allen, 'tell him your plans.' It may be reassuring or disturbing to think that God controls the smallest details of our lives, but it does raise a number of serious questions.

There is first the question of perspective. What are we to think about a God who finds a parking space for one person but fails to prevent a horrendous motorway crash in which thirty people are killed? How are we to understand a God who saves one person from death by making him miss the train, while allowing his three friends, along with many other people, to be killed? What is God doing when he finds a bed so that a Christian can have a minor operation, but allows thousands of children to die of starvation in other parts of the world?

Closely related to this, there is, secondly, the question of human freedom. Freedom is essential to any truly personal relationship. God is love, and if we are to love God in return, we must be free to do so. God's will and purpose make demands on us, and we choose whether or not to respond, whether to obey or disobey. The possibility of a personal relationship depends on that free choice. Without it, we would be machines with God pulling the levers, computers with God writing the programme.

It is therefore possible, and inevitable, that God's will is often frustrated by our disobedience. We have the resources and the technology to make sure that literally no one on this earth is hungry. We do not have the will. The gap between rich and poor, not merely between countries but within them, grows ever wider. Human freedom and sinfulness may not always be the immediate cause of starvation, but they are entirely responsible for the failure to remedy it. It is hard to believe that God intervenes personally and directly to provide one person with a convenient parking space while evidently doing nothing directly to provide food for the hungry.

Thirdly, human freedom is bound up with the question of our maturity and responsibility. There is a dependence on God which is simple in the best sense, uncomplicated and deep, which recognizes the power of divine love and the reality of human freedom. John Bayley, in his memoir of Iris Murdoch, talks about 'growing closer and closer apart'. The phrase describes vividly the maturity of a deep personal relationship. The belief that God is constantly intervening to smooth the path of his children, and that we have to rely on God to tell us what to do and when and how may lead to a dependence which is not mature and responsible, but childish.

Fourthly, there is the question of our interdependence. The bridge player, whose run of poor cards taught him patience and perspective, was playing with a partner who also had to endure his misfortune. David Attenborough's opportunity came at the expense of the man who fell seriously ill. The fact that one person finds a convenient parking space means that another person, who might have needed it more, does not.

The lives of individuals, families, communities and whole countries are interconnected in a myriad ways. My sinfulness may have disastrous consequences for someone else. If God intervenes directly on my behalf and for my convenience, the results may be distinctly inconvenient for another person; unless, of course, God is thought to intervene on their behalf too, in which case, human freedom quickly becomes meaningless.

Fifthly, it may be suggested that God works for good only with those who love him; but that too is fraught with problems. It makes God out to be a tribal god, concerned only, or primarily, with those who belong to him and neglectful of everyone else. In the earliest days of the people of Israel, when they were a tribal society ruled by judges, they believed that there were many gods. Their God, so they believed, was stronger than the others, and if they were loyal, their God would defeat their enemies and keep them safe. Gideon's 300 men win a famous victory, but at the expense of the slaughter of thousands of the Midianites, a slaughter with which God is thought to be well pleased.

It is by means of a long, winding path of discovery, through many generations, that we have come to believe that there is one God, and that God's love and will embrace every human being. But there is always the temptation to revert to tribal beliefs, to claim that our God is for us and against them. The story of civilization is, from one point of view, the detribalizing of society, and the recognition that slaves, blacks, women and gays are all created equal.

This means that chance occurrences happen equally to anyone and everyone. One person frequently finds that as he drives down the road, someone pulls out and leaves him a convenient place to park. Others are never so lucky. Being a Christian seems to make little difference. Lucky breaks in work, chance happenings which are life-changing, are not restricted to Christians. They can and do happen to anyone. So does misfortune.

Illness is not confined to those who are wicked. Accidents happen to those who do not deserve them, as well as to those who do.

This catalogue of questions and comments leads me to one clear conclusion, though I recognize that it will not be shared by some sincere and committed Christians. The idea that God is constantly intervening, directly and personally, to help and support individual people, is simply unbelievable. There are, as I have tried to indicate, far too many problems attached to it.

A man who got himself into a difficult situation prayed desperately to God for help. He heard a voice saying to him, 'You got yourself into this mess, you get yourself out of it!' In the 1930s, the father of a large American family was saying grace before their Thanksgiving meal. His long, rambling prayer embraced in some detail all the members of the family, who were living in various parts of the States, and then concluded, 'There's no need for you to worry your head about our Jack – he's here and we can look after him ourselves.'

Belief in divine providence does not mean that God is in direct personal control of every aspect of our lives, nor that God looks after whatever we cannot manage by ourselves. But there are two other possibilities. One is that God has so ordered the universe and the natural world that, in a sense, everything is taken care of. The world is created in such a way that there are endless possibilities, and chance, coincidence and accident are all an integral part of that world. What happens today is either a result of natural laws, or is a direct consequence of what happened yesterday, or is the choice and action of human freedom. God does not intervene personally and directly. God's providence lies in the providential ordering of the universe.

The problem, of course, with this point of view is that it so affirms the independence of the world that divine control in effect disappears. God becomes the clock-maker who winds up the clock and sets it going, but then watches passively while it runs its course. Since we have concluded, in the previous two chapters, that neither the natural world nor the course of history is all predetermined, and that human beings have free will, on this view the world would quickly be out of God's control altogether.

The second point of view suggests that God's providence consists entirely in guiding people's response to events. This view takes us back to the principle of complementarity. Faith in God transfigures what happens, both the ordinary and the extraordinary, by lifting them into a higher and larger context. It is as if a person who lived in the two dimensions of length and breadth became aware of depth. Or as if a person who was colour-blind began to see colours. The same objects, the same people, would be seen in a quite different light, with an added dimension.

To the person who prays for a parking space, and finds one, that is a sign of God's care in the smallest details of life, a reassuring sign and a cause for thanksgiving. To a person with no faith, the fact that there is a convenient space is simply a coincidence.

Two people look at a beautiful rose bush. One sees the hand of God and gives thanks. The other sees a work of nature and enjoys it. Two people are saved from death by the narrowest of margins. One thanks

God, the other thanks his lucky stars. Two people have an exceptionally long and bad run of cards. One concludes that God is in it, teaching him. The other either loses patience altogether, and gives up playing; or sits it out, knowing that on the law of averages, his luck will turn.

A man goes to work on the same train every morning. He is in the habit of praying before he begins the day, and on this particular morning, he prays for patience. He either lingers too long over his breakfast or the train is early, because he arrives at the station a few seconds too late. He stamps impatiently up and down the platform until he suddenly remembers his prayer; and then he realises that missing the train is God's answer. For how could he learn patience unless God gave him opportunity to do so?

God did not make him delay over his breakfast, nor make the train driver leave the platform early. It is, of course, possible that he prayed for patience so earnestly that he spent too long over it and so missed the train; but that was his fault. In this case, God's providence is evident in the man's response to events. Because he had prayed for patience, he was more likely to interpret what happened as God's answer; and if he learned patience, that itself would have an impact on the way he related to other people and so on the future course of events.

On this view, every event is a result of natural law, human freedom, what has already happened before, chance and coincidence; but what matters is how we respond to events, and whether we do so in co-operation with God. To a person who believes in God, nothing happens by chance and nothing is ever mere coincidence.

Everything that happens – literally everything, good or bad, accident or will – is raw material to be woven into a personal relationship with God. Clearly there is a great deal of truth in this view. This seems to be precisely what St Paul meant when he said that 'In everything, God works for good with those who love him.'

The question is whether this belief goes far enough. It makes the action of God wholly dependent on people's response, and seems to exclude the possibility that God might take any direct initiative. Yet the story of God's dealings with people, from first to last, is an account of divine initiative. 'The Lord said to Abraham, Leave your country, your relatives and your father's home, and go to a land that I am going to show you.' 'When the time had fully come, God sent forth his Son, born of a woman . . .'[7] 'God is not merely responding to events, nor waiting for other people to respond. God makes things happen. The experience of people of faith, down the ages, is one of response to God's initiative.

How is it possible, then, to say that God does not intervene directly to control the detailed events of people's lives, while at the same time affirming that God takes the initiative? It is at this point that we have to distinguish between God's 'normal' providential action and what is sometimes called 'special providence'. Normal providence is God working through the natural world and natural laws, and through people's response to what happens. 'Special providence' is God taking direct initiative.

Very often, what we describe as 'special providence' is in fact God working through natural causes and other people and chance, in a way which has special results.

Two people meet quite by chance, they fall in love, marry and enjoy great happiness together. It is likely, if they are both Christians, that they will describe the circumstances of their meeting as special. It was meant, they say, implying that God had a direct hand in it. In a sense they are right, because God is responsible for a world in which such chance encounters happen. But this is really 'normal providence' with special results.

Normally, everything that happens is connected backwards through time to what has happened before. The chain of cause and effect, for good or ill, is unbroken. But there are some events which are different. They break into the normal course of events with sudden and dramatic urgency. They are divine initiatives. God calls, or acts, in a way which is neither miraculous nor, strictly speaking, normal. The call of Abraham and the conversion of St Paul are two obvious examples; but special providence is, in my view, rare.

If C. S. Lewis is right, special providence does not happen at all. There is either normal providence, or there is miracle, but there is no in-between. There is what happens normally, through natural laws, where every event interlocks with every other; and there are rare miraculous events which are divine interventions. Miracles are special acts of God, but everything else is equally providential. Natural laws, natural causes and providence are not alternatives because all are one. 'If God directs the course of events at all, then he directs the movement of every atom at every moment.' Certainly there is free will, but that is within the ultimate control of the divine will.[8]

Lewis argues that God is outside time, and therefore

all events are eternally present to God. He compares God to a designer, who draws a perfect pattern of inter-locking lines, so intricate and complete that when you or I reach a certain point in our lives, and make choices by our own free will, both the situation and the choice are known to God and the pattern is already arranged accordingly.

It is difficult to imagine God outside time, with every decision, every event, every person, eternally there. It is even more difficult to think logically about a dimension of timelessness in which we do not live and of which we have no experience. It may be because of this that Lewis finds himself talking, without any apparent awareness of contradiction, of God being outside time and creating the universe 'at this minute – at every minute'.

The way in which Lewis speaks about this creation sounds to me like another form of determinism. The pattern is arranged in the eternal mind of God before I get there. Hence there is either the pre-arranged pattern, or there are direct, miraculous interventions, but no 'special' acts of God, since everything is special.

The situation at Dunkirk is often quoted as an example of special providence. The calm weather, which allowed much of the British army to escape across the Channel, was held to be an act of God in answer to prayer. But, writes Lewis, either the weather was exactly what the previous course of the weather and natural forces would have produced, in which case there was no special providence; or God controlled the weather and made it calm, in which case it was a miracle. In this particular case, Lewis' logic is right.

The call of Abraham, though, is not a natural event

which can be explained by natural law or historical forces. It was an act of God. But it was not a miracle. Special providence is a phrase which describes those events which are not miraculous, but which are caused by the direct action of God.

Most of us, I suggest, do not experience special providence. We experience a complex network of cause and effect, which, from one point of view, is entirely natural, and from another, the perspective of faith, is all of God. A tile blows off a roof, and this time it is not a passer-by who is killed. The tile injures me. It is an accident. I understand something of the complex causes, the wind currents, the fact that sometimes builders fix tiles with nails which rust away.

I do not believe that the tile fell because God planned it and made it happen. In that sense, it is not the will of God. But as a person of faith, I also recognize that everything that happens is somehow within the care and purpose of God, and can be made to serve God's good will. In that sense, it is God's will.

I may argue that though God did not make it happen, God did allow it to happen; but that only pushes the question one stage further back. If I allow something to happen when I could have prevented it, that is not so very different from making it happen. If I believe in God at all, I accept the mystery: that through natural causes, a tile falls and injures me, which is not God's will; but because God is the source of all that is, and because he can make even wind-blown tiles to serve the ultimate good, it is God's will.

The journalist T. E. Utley went completely blind at the age of nine. His son once wrote that

God seemed to me to have dealt him an especially cruel hand. I always thought it particularly unfair that the disease which blinded him also caused him terrible headaches. Bad enough not to be able to see, I thought, but unspeakably cruel that his useless eyes should also hurt him. Yet all this he accepted without fuss as the mysterious will of God, while remaining witty and worldly until his dying day.

Utley seems to have gone beyond thinking of his blindness as allowed by God, into accepting it as the will of God. But he surely cannot have meant that his blindness was caused by God; any more than God deliberately made Beethoven deaf. There were natural causes for both afflictions. But they were not outside the will of God, and were part of God's providential ordering of the world. In that sense, they could be accepted, by faith, as 'the mysterious will of God'.

The most striking expression of faith in this mystery is the saying of Job, 'The Lord gave and the Lord has taken away. Blessed be the name of the Lord.'[9] Originally spoken after a series of horrendous catastrophes, those words are sometimes uttered when a person has died. From one point of view, it was a human act of procreation which gave life and it was a virus or a disease, a road accident or old age, which took life away. From the perspective of faith, it is God who gives life through human procreation, and it is God's doing that disease, accident and old age cause death; and both life and death are part of God's good will and purpose. To hold both points of view at the same time is to have faith in the mystery of divine providence.

Some suggestions for reflection

In all things, God works together for good with those who love him, those who are called according to his purpose. (Romans 8:28) All nature is but art unknown to thee, all chance direction which thou canst not see. (Alexander Pope)

Have you had any experiences of luck or chance which have affected your life? How do you understand such experiences?

Does God ever find parking places, and if so who for and why?

Is it reasonable, and do you think it right, to suggest that one event could be at the same time a natural occurrence, and contrary to the will of God, and part of God's providential care?

Chapter 4

It's a Miracle

So far we have focused on normal or special providence, and have made only passing reference to miracle. Miracles are an integral part of divine providence and they are significant in all religious experience. Accounts of the miracles performed, or said to have been performed by Jesus, take up almost a third of the Gospel records.

For some people, talk of miracle quickens the pulse. This is what religion is really about – God doing dramatic things. If God heals the sick, makes the blind see, feeds the hungry, then we can be sure of God's existence and intentions.

But if miracles are invested with such extravagant expectations, the reality is bound to be a disappointment; and even without such high hopes, miracles, after the first excitement, tend to fade away into anti-climax. Jesus Christ, Superstar, is invited by Herod to 'Prove to me that you're no fool, Walk across my swimming pool.' But Jesus refused to perform miracles 'on demand', and expressed disappointment at people's failure to understand them. 'Do not work for food which goes bad,' he said; 'instead, work for the food that lasts for eternal life.'[1]

Even bread provided miraculously goes stale and mouldy in time. The lepers were healed, but later, inevitably, they became sick and died. Poor Lazarus, brought back from the dead, had to do his dying all over again. Miracles, even the most dramatic of them, are quickly absorbed into nature. They must have a significance beyond the immediate event and a meaning which survives the first flush of excitement; otherwise, they can seem like cruel conjuring tricks.

Some years ago, in the early 1970s, an Englishman visited one of the poorest parts of Chile. He is a thoughtful, somewhat sceptical man, with a delightful sense of humour, not given to exaggeration, and not likely to believe anything he has not experienced for himself. He told of visiting a tiny church, with room for fifty, crowded with three times that number. Towards the end of a long and dynamic act of worship, the pastor and the evangelist invite those who need healing to pray for it, and to put their hands where they need healing. Most of the people touch their teeth. The diet is so poor that most suffer from agonizing tooth decay.

Prayer for healing is offered and those whose prayer is answered are invited to show what has happened. The Englishman wrote:

Because the Evangelist sees in me a sceptical European, I am summoned to the platform to see for myself the works of God. Doubting Thomas is not allowed to lurk in a corner. With the assistance of the Evangelist's torch (who, expecting great things from God, has come prepared) I look into their mouths, one after the other. And I know that what I see is a miracle. For these folk never go to the dentist. The poor of Chile are poor beyond our imagination and dental treatment is entirely beyond their means. But these teeth have been filled, and the filling has the form of a silver cross set in each tooth.[2]

To the people, such miracles were a sign, a reminder of the fact that God loved them and had not forsaken them, despite all the evidence to the contrary. But the miracle did not solve everything. The people needed food more than fillings, a balanced diet that would prevent tooth decay; and that was not given. The people needed justice more than mercy, a society in which their labour would receive a fair reward, and that was not given. Even the teeth, so miraculously filled, would decay again. The people rejoiced in the miracle, as the act of a loving God, and the relief from pain was exhilarating. They went out of the church, their faith strengthened, into a harsh and unchanged world.

The word 'miracle' is almost irretrievably lost to us. It is used with such lack of precision that it can mean almost anything or nothing. 'Don't expect miracles!' we warn, as a way of lowering expectations. A person escapes without harm from a nasty car accident, and it is said to be 'miraculous'. Two people are buried in an avalanche, and dug out after three days, alive and unhurt. Their survival is described as 'a miracle'. England's cricketers, facing another desperate situation, are frequently said to be in need of a miracle. Even the dramatic recovery of the stock-market is occasionally described as 'miraculous'.

Strictly speaking, a miracle is an occasion for wonder.

It is an awe-inspiring event. It reveals a supernatural being. The use of the word 'miracle' to describe what happened to the people in Chile was precise and accurate. A miracle is, to quote the *Oxford Dictionary*, 'A marvellous event exceeding the known powers of nature, and therefore supposed to be due to the special intervention of the Deity or of some supernatural agency.' Miracles are signs. They point to a reality greater than what is either natural or expected.

Apart from the miracle of the resurrection of Jesus, the miracle which is most extensively reported in the New Testament is the feeding of the five thousand. All four Gospels give an account of it at some length, and for good measure, Matthew and Mark both record the feeding of the four thousand as well. The feeding of the five thousand was thought to be so significant that it is deeply embedded in the earliest traditions of the Christian community, so much so that by the time the Gospels were written down, several versions of the miracle were in circulation, all slightly different.

A careful reading of the text seems to indicate that the feedings of the four and of the five thousand are two versions of the same miracle. Matthew and Mark record the feeding of the five thousand first, and then the feeding of the four thousand. St Luke follows St Mark's account up to verse 45 of chapter 6, where the feeding of the five thousand ends; and then he breaks off, and returns to St Mark after the end of the feeding of the four thousand. Either St Luke has decided to leave out material in St Mark which he considered repetitious, or he is using an older version which does not include the feeding of the four thousand. St John tells only of the feeding of the five thousand, and he uses a tradition which is different from the other three.

The story raises sharply the two primary questions concerning miracles: do they happen, and if so, what do they mean?

It used to be fashionable, particularly in schools, to tell the story of the feeding of the five thousand as if it were a morality tale about sharing. This great crowd of people has been with Jesus for three days. They are all feeling hungry, but no one gets any food out because no one else does; so no one knows whether there is enough to go round. Then Jesus is told about the boy who has five loaves and two fish. He takes the food, blesses it, breaks it, and tells the people to share it. With wry smiles, people take out the food they have brought. Everyone shares, everyone eats, and there is so much food that there are twelve baskets full of left-overs. Jesus has persuaded the people to share. It is a miracle.

Told in this way, it is, of course, nothing of the sort. It is just a great picnic, easily explained, which reveals that Jesus is a moderately capable leader. A miracle is an extraordinary event for which there is no natural explanation. It involves rather more than persuading people to share the food they have brought.

Such explanations belong to a time when miracles were thought to be impossible, and they are a legacy of the philosopher David Hume. In 1748, his famous *Enquiry concerning Human Understanding* was published, and Part Ten, 'Of Miracles', concluded simply that miracles do not happen. The uniformity of nature means that miracles are extremely improbable; so improbable, in fact, that it is more probable that the witnesses who claim to have seen one are either mistaken or lying.

This dogmatic denial of miracles led to an attempt to retain the miracles in the Bible by giving them natural explanations, and some of the explanations are less credible, or less honest, than the miracles themselves. Jesus is said, on one occasion, to have walked on the water. There are some who believe that he did, and that this was a miracle indicating that Jesus is supreme over the natural world. There are others who hold that he did not, and that the story is a legend, told to emphasize the power of Jesus. There is a third view, the natural explanation, which suggests that Jesus was actually wading in the surf, but due to an optical illusion, the disciples thought he was walking on the water, and that it was a miracle. The first two views are credible. The third, it seems to me, is dishonest. It attempts to retain the significance of the miracle while at the same time explaining it away.

There are two main reasons for the assertion that miracles do not happen. One is that nature does not allow them. The second is that some who believe sincerely in God nonetheless think that God would not work miracles.

It is said that nature does not allow them because the laws of nature are unalterable. The sun always rises in the east and cannot rise anywhere else. Heat warms and ice makes cold. To reverse them would be both impossible and stupid. What seem to us to be miracles are simply due to our failure to understand more about the way in which nature works. If we knew more, we would eventually recognize that everything which once seemed miraculous could be attributed to natural causes.

People believed that Jesus performed miracles, it is argued, because they did not understand enough about the natural world. They knew, from experience and observation, that there is a pattern in nature, but they understood little about how nature works. To them, everything was the work of the creator God, who had set the stars in their courses, but could as easily move them. Sudden and dramatic alterations to the regular pattern of nature were miracles, but like the growth of corn and the warmth of the sun, they were all equally the acts of the creator God.

Today, some people of faith believe that miracles are entirely consistent with the natural world, and are, as it were, fed into nature. A miracle is, by definition, an act of God, but the mechanism of a miracle, so to speak, may be God acting in nature to cause a different pattern at a specific time.

A miracle may interrupt the course of nature, but it is absorbed by nature with remarkable speed. Bread provided miraculously is eaten and digested. The lame man who is cured, after an initial burst of leaping and dancing, settles down to walk again. People who are dramatically healed do, in the end, die. All this may lend weight to the argument that if only we knew more about nature, we would find that there are no miracles at all, only natural causes and coincidences of timing.

But at the tomb of Lazarus, the argument that miracles do not contravene the laws of nature breaks down. The account in St John's Gospel tells us that Lazarus had been dead for four days. To emphasize the point, we are also told of his sister's horrified reaction when Jesus asks for the tomb to be opened. 'There will be a bad smell,' says the *Good News Bible*, prosaically. 'Peradventure he stinketh' may be archaic, but is far more telling.[3]

If Lazarus was in fact brought back from the dead, then this miracle does contravene the pattern of nature. This reverses the natural process of death and decay. From the moment of birth, it is said, we are in decline, and our bodies are constantly renewing themselves; but each renewal is a little less effective than the last, until the whole process comes to an end in death. Lazarus was not raised to a new order of being. The Gospel makes it clear that he was brought back to this life. Not to put too fine a point on it, rotting flesh and decaying organs were made whole again. If this is what actually happened, it was, in the proper sense of the word, unnatural; some would say, impossible. It was not a suspension of nature, nor an interruption, but a denial of nature.

In the natural world, everything moves steadily forwards in a pattern of death and new life, and everything in life is connected backwards to everything else. This is why life is sometimes said to be 'one damn thing after another'. A person is ill with food poisoning because he ate something that had gone off; and it had gone off because it was kept a day longer than it should have been, and that was because a guest who was invited for Sunday lunch did not arrive, so there was food left over, and so on backwards through an unending chain of cause and effect.

Miracles are not connected backwards through a chain of cause and effect. They break that continuous chain. Even if they do not contradict nature, they do transcend the known laws of nature. If nature and history were determined in advance, then miracles could not happen. But we have already argued that both the natural world and human life are all the time open to endless possibilities. What are called the laws of nature are not absolutely unalterable. Human beings have genuine freedom of choice. In theory, at least, miracles – even a miracle such as the raising of Lazarus – are possible. In the end, we may discover that what we thought were miracles were all due to natural causes; but that would not destroy the faith of a person who believes that everything, whether natural or miraculous, is of God.

Of course, if there is no God, no supernatural agency, then there is nothing beyond or outside nature, and no possibility of miracle. But to believe in God does not automatically include belief in miracles. The god who is a life-force – elemental, impersonal energy – will not perform miracles. The god who is evident wherever there is beauty or truth or goodness, who exists in our appreciation of beauty, could not create miracle. The god who is our own best self, the ideal vision of what we consider to be the highest and best in human life, would be as incapable of miracle as we are ourselves.

The God in whom Christians believe does not exist inside our own souls, as energy or beauty or aspiration. God is over against us, a personal God, the creator of all that is. God is pictured as father and mother, shepherd, king, hunter, lover. God invites, commands, calls, demands, rebukes and encourages. God's voice is the still, small voice and also the voice of thunder from the heavens. God is our refuge and strength and also a consuming fire.

By the word of the Lord the heavens were made. It is a small thing that the Lord, by a word, should cause a miracle to happen. But what God can do and what God chooses to do are not at all the same. Is not power exercised most effectively, not by using it, but by limiting its use? Why would God, who has created a regular pattern in nature, choose to break it? It is a poor workman who finishes the job, and then has to tinker with it. Miracles are unpredictable and capricious. They create more problems than they solve. You might expect miracles of the old Greek gods, who needed to demonstrate their power and keep people on their toes, uncertain of what might happen next; but such tricks are somehow unworthy of God.

These are strong objections which persuade many people of sincere faith that God does not work miracles. It is true that the person who understands power is the one who respects its limitations. A good driver in a powerful car will not hurtle along at full throttle; but it is the accelerator rather than the brake that is most likely to correct a sudden skid. A great artist knows and respects the rules of his craft, and may have spent many years learning technique; but a great artist is more likely than a mediocre one to break those rules in the pursuit of a greater unity. The car manufacturer whose cars have to be tinkered with to get them right is a bad car-maker; but the created world is not like a machine, whose maker can justly be blamed if parts are missing. It is more like a garden – growing, developing and needing constant attention.

It's a Miracle

The argument which seems to me to have most force is that miracles are arbitrary, more like the capricious acts of a god than the purposeful acts of God. Bartimaeus, a blind beggar, just happens to be sitting at the roadside when Jesus is passing. He is healed. But there are fifty other blind men and women in Galilee. They are not healed. Teeth are miraculously filled in one church in Chile, but not in another. There is a detailed report in the medical journal, *The Lancet*, of a patient making a full recovery from cancer that cannot be explained by any medical reason. The doctors are puzzled, though not altogether surprised, since such accounts are rare but well attested. But in the same hospital there is a young mother, a Christian, also suffering from cancer, praying and longing for a miracle. She dies.

It seems that either there must be no miracles at all; or there must be miracles all the time and for everyone; or miracles must appear arbitrary. If God never worked miracles, then the problem of them appearing arbitrary or capricious would, of course, disappear. But miracles are such well-attested events in human history that only the most determined and dogmatic bigotry could deny them totally.

If there were miracles all the time, for everyone, then the world would be utterly different. It would mean that we were all the time subject to divine intervention. We might be given freedom to choose whether or not to accept a miracle, but who would refuse? Freedom, and with it personal relationships and growth into human maturity, would all be hopelessly corrupted. The regularity of the natural world would gradually be eroded; and if we did not know whether fire would boil water or freeze it, we could never enjoy even a cup of tea.

If miracles happen at all, then, they must be rare, and so must appear arbitrary. That does not mean that they are purposeless. Why one person is miraculously healed from cancer and another not is no different from the question, 'Why did this person get cancer in the first place while that other person did not?' The real question raised by miraculous healing is, 'Why has this person's death been postponed?'

Miracles are not the capricious acts of a playful god. They are consistent with the character of God, and they are signs, pointing to the reality of God. They are acts of generosity by a loving creator. There are therefore two ways of assessing accounts of miracles. First, are they consistent with the character of God? And second, do they mean something which is consistent with the rest of the Christian revelation?

The apocryphal gospels contain stories about Jesus which were thought untrue or unsuitable by the writers of the four Gospels. One story tells of Jesus as a child making models of birds out of clay, and then breathing on them: and the birds immediately came to life and flew away. The story is of a boy performing conjuring tricks for his own amusement. It is inconsistent with the character of God and has no meaning.

There are two miracle stories in the Gospels which seem to me similar. One is not really a miracle at all. It is a joke. The disciples tell Jesus that they owe some tax, and Jesus tells them to 'go to the lake and drop in a line. Pull up the first fish you hook, and in its mouth you will find a coin worth enough for my temple tax and yours.'[4] Though the story was sometimes understood as a miracle, it is more likely that Jesus' comment was met with a burst of laughter from the disciples. Today, hundreds of pilgrims lunch at Ein Gev, the kibbutz on the shores of Galilee, and they are all offered 'St Peter's fish', which has colouring on the sides of its head which vaguely resembles a shekel.

The other strange miracle, which we considered briefly earlier, is the account of Jesus walking on the water. The story is included in Matthew, Mark and John, and all place it as the sequel to the feeding of the five thousand. St John's account is much shorter and lacks the drama of the other two, but it has more meaning. For John, the heart of the story is Jesus saying the same words by which the greatest sayings in the Gospel are introduced: 'I am the bread of life . . . the light of the world . . .' and so on, except that in this story the words are simply 'I am'. They can mean simply 'It's me, don't be afraid.' But John implies more. 'I am' is the name for God, and this miracle is a revelation of the divinity of Jesus.

It is also perhaps linked to the Passover, which is so prominent in the rest of the chapter. Just as the children of Israel ate the Passover meal and then miraculously crossed the Red Sea, so Jesus provides food for the people, and then walks across the Sea of Galilee. That may explain the extra comment in St Mark, which the other two leave out, that Jesus 'would have passed by' the boat; and presumably, if the terrified disciples had not called out to him, he would have walked straight across the sea to the other side.

The story may also be read as an anticipation of the resurrection. If so, it is a glimpse of the new creation, a hint of what will be possible in the new resurrection body. There is no shortage of meaning that can be attached to the story, much of it convincing.

For many people, that meaning, the fact that the story is included in the New Testament, and that the writers of the Gospels thought it was a miracle, is enough. Who are we to impose our modern scepticism on the story, and decide that it could not have happened? What would the disciples or the writers of the Gospels have gained from inventing the story?

Others will find questions hard to suppress. This miracle is the only one, apart from the raising of Lazarus, which clearly and directly contravenes the laws of nature. Since the body of Jesus had not been changed by the resurrection, and the sea was still the same, he should have sunk to the bottom. If he was intending a glimpse of the new nature in advance of the resurrection, he does not say so, and the disciples missed the point. They were simply terrified.

If Jesus really intended to walk past the boat, was he just taking the quickest route across the sea instead of walking all the way round? It is highly unlikely that he would do something so uncharacteristically self-indulgent. There is something odd about this miracle. It does not fit into the rest of Jesus' ministry. John Baker suggests that 'the feel is reminiscent of tales from other sources about divine visitants in disguise, as though Jesus knew that he could perform these wonders any time he wanted to, but used the power only occasionally as a gesture of kindness or simply for a bit of fun'.[5] The disciples did not see the joke.

My own view, for what it is worth, is that after feeding

the five thousand, Jesus went away on his own, and then walked round the sea and rejoined the disciples on the other side. They, meanwhile, had crossed over by boat. Later, after the death and resurrection of Jesus, the feeding of the five thousand was seen in the light of the Passover. The Jewish *Haggadah*, the narrative recited at the Passover meal, links together closely the gift of manna and the crossing of the Red Sea. So the first Christians added to the feeding miracle a story of Jesus miraculously crossing the Sea of Galilee, to complete the parallel. That seems to me much more likely than that Jesus actually walked across it.

The miracle of the feeding of the five thousand is a different matter. That miracle does not break the laws of nature. It transcends them in a way that is wholly fitting. To turn stones into bread, as Jesus was tempted to do in the wilderness, would have been to break the laws of nature. To turn a little bread into many loaves, or two fish into enough to feed a multitude, is what God is constantly doing in the natural world. It is usually described, in harvest festival sermons, as nature's prodigality. Sow one bean, and a plant grows which produces a hundred beans. Bury a seed of corn in the earth, and first the blade appears, then the ear, then the full corn. The miracle is wholly consistent with the character of God.

But Jesus was not giving a demonstration of his power over creation, nor a lesson in God's generosity. Although he feeds hungry people, the miracle is not intended to give an early impetus to the work of Christian Aid. The miracle has a deeper meaning that is entirely consistent with the rest of Christian revelation, though it was at first seriously misunderstood.

Strange Design

The accounts in the Gospels of Matthew, Mark and Luke tell us that the people were with Jesus all day. Towards evening, the disciples asked Jesus to send them away so that they could buy food and get shelter for the night. John's account is different. He tells us that Jesus went away from the crowd, and then they found him again and came towards him in great numbers. As soon as he saw them coming, Jesus decided that he would feed them. It was, John reminds us, close to the Jewish feast of the Passover.

The boy with five loaves and two fish was found, and Jesus told the disciples to make the people sit down. Mark and Luke add the interesting detail that Jesus wanted them seated 'by companies'. The word which Mark uses means literally 'in ranks'. It is used to describe straight rows of leeks. The people were not in groups, like picnickers. They might have been lined up to form a hollow square. It was more like military manoeuvres than a day out.

John tells us that there were about five thousand present, but the other three writers make a point of the fact that there were five thousand men, 'not counting the women and children'. The men would fight.

Jesus then took the bread and the loaves, blessed them, broke them and gave them to the people. At the end of the meal, when everyone had eaten enough, someone counted the baskets full of scraps. There was one for each of the twelve tribes of Israel.

Slowly it dawned on the people that this was the great banquet which God had promised, the feast which the Messiah would give; 'as it is written, he gave them bread from heaven to eat'.[6] Matthew, Mark and Luke tell us that the feast ended suddenly, when Jesus ordered his disciples to get into a boat. The word 'ordered' is particularly strong. He made them do it, so that he would be alone, without his 'officers'. Then, with supreme authority, he dismissed the crowd.

John tells us why. The people wanted to make him a king, by force. They wanted a champion to lead them against the Romans. They thought that Jesus was the political and military Messiah they had so longed for. What Jesus had intended as a sign of God's kingdom had gone wrong. The people had misunderstood. So he dismissed them and went away by himself to pray.

Later, perhaps much later, the Christians came to realise the true purpose of the miracle. In St John's Gospel, after the crossing of the sea, the feeding is the basis for a long discourse on the bread of life. This is the real meaning of the miracle. Jesus said, 'I am the bread of life. The one who comes to me will never go hungry; the one who believes in me will never be thirsty.'[7]

At the time of Passover, Jesus fed the people with bread from heaven. It was the promised heavenly feast, offered to the people by God's chosen Messiah. 'I am the living bread that came down from heaven,' Jesus said. 'If anyone eats this bread, he will live for ever. The bread that I will give him is my flesh, which I give so that the world may live.'[8]

At another Passover meal, Jesus again took bread, and blessed, and broke and gave. The first part of the bread of life teaching focuses on believing in the Messiah (John 6:35–50), the second half is about eating the bread. The feeding of the five thousand anticipates the Eucharist. Jesus said to them, 'I am telling you the truth, whoever eats my flesh and drinks my blood has eternal life' (John 6:53–54).

It is only in St John's Gospel that the miracles are described as signs. They might equally be described as sacraments. They make great spiritual truth real and tangible. Miracles are, of necessity, rare. They neither break nor suspend what are called the laws of nature. They interrupt the course of nature and are quickly absorbed. They are the occasional acts of a generous providence, reminders that all of life and the whole of creation is in the care of a loving, personal God.

> Earth's crammed with heaven,
> And every common bush afire with God;
> But only he who sees, takes off his shoes,
> The rest sit round it and pluck blackberries . . .[9]

Some suggestions for reflection

This beginning of miracles did Jesus in Cana of Galilee, and manifested forth his glory; and his disciples believed on him. (John 2:11)
Jesus sighed deeply in his spirit and said, 'Why does this generation seek a sign. Truly I say to you, no sign shall be given to this generation.' (Mark 8:12)

Do you have any direct, personal experience of the miraculous power of God, and if so, how do you understand or explain it?

It's a Miracle

'Miracles are, of necessity, rare.' True or false?

Do you think it more likely that Jesus walked on
the water, or that the first Christians added to the
account of the feeding of the five thousand an
account of Jesus miraculously crossing the sea, to
complete the parallel with the Exodus?

Chapter 5

'Take This Cup From Me'

The cricket match was slowly coming to a predictable and boring end. The other team needed to score over thirty runs to win, and had three more wickets in hand. There was one over left. I was fielding at deep extra cover, and to relieve the boredom, I decided to turn the game into an experiment in prayer. I was thirteen at the time, with a modest curiosity about religion. I began to pray that the last three batsmen would be out and that our team would win.

The first three balls were bowled without incident. I went on praying. The fourth ball removed the batsman's middle stump. Two balls were left, and two batsmen. The fifth ball was well hit and equally well caught. One ball left and one batsman. I prayed harder. The last ball was bowled, and the batsman played it gently back up the wicket. Match drawn. But suddenly, in a burst of madness, the batsman shouted, 'Run!' and set off. His partner stood still, too shocked to move. The batsman was run out by the full length of the pitch.

The fact that the boredom of a cricket match had been relieved by a religious experiment, and that we had won the match, was eclipsed by the rather alarming thought that my prayers might have influenced the result. The possibility that God might have done something for a thirteen-year-old schoolboy was both exciting and worrying.

My prayer had the single merit of innocence, though an innocence largely rooted in ignorance. It was an entirely selfish prayer. Worse still, it was an experiment, a childish attempt to discover proof that God exists. Today, I think the dramatic end of the cricket match was a coincidence; either that, or God has a sense of humour. Though I find it difficult to believe in a God who would make one poor batsman run simply in order to satisfy my whims.

The prayer which asks God to make certain things happen is the most basic form of prayer and also the most problematic. Prayer as communion, as waiting on God, the prayer of silence and contemplation is a form of prayer which is easy to justify though difficult to practise. The prayer of worship and of thanksgiving is a natural expression of an awareness of God. But asking God to do things for us or for other people is, on the face of it, absurd.

'Do not be anxious about anything,' writes St Paul, 'but in everything, by prayer and supplication, with thanksgiving, let your requests be made known to God.'[1] Prayers which take literally the phrase 'make known to God' point up the apparent absurdity. Prayers for healing sometimes include a detailed description of symptoms, a diagnosis, and suggestions for a cure. 'You know, O Lord' is often the prelude to a prayer which contains a large amount of intimate information about other people. Leave aside the unworthy thought that in public prayer meetings, this might be 'spiritual' gossiping.

Jesus himself said that 'Your Heavenly Father knows that you need all these things.' So why did Jesus tell us to pray, 'Give us this day our daily bread'?

When we pray for someone who is about to have a heart bypass operation, what are we doing? Are we attempting to persuade an all-powerful God to change the course of events so that the surgeons are on top form and the operation is successful? Are we giving information to an all-knowing God, to ensure that the date and time of the operation are included in the heavenly diary? Are we providing a reminder to an all-loving God, lest by some chance the operation might be outside that love? Or are we using prayer as a way of coming to terms with reality, and preparing ourselves to cope, whatever the outcome? Just to put the question in these ways invites the mockery to which Elijah subjected the prophets of Baal: 'Pray louder! He is a god! Maybe he is day-dreaming or relieving himself, or perhaps he's gone on a journey! Or maybe he's sleeping, and you've got to wake him up!'[2]

What do we think we are doing when we ask God to do specific things? The answer to this question reveals what we think about God and what we think about ourselves. Prayer is the acid test of belief. What we think and do about prayer tells more clearly than anything else what we believe about God and what we believe about ourselves in relation to God.

To speak of God in personal terms, as loving, caring, speaking, listening, does not mean that God is a person. The word 'person' was used in the early Church in its struggles to understand and express its experience of God. The Christians had come to know God as Father,

Son and Holy Spirit, and this had somehow to be reconciled with the hard-won belief that there is one God.
The word they eventually settled on was the Latin word
persona, which described the mask worn by actors.

Bishop David Jenkins once remarked that the doctrine
of the Trinity is easy, provided that you remember that
three does not mean three, one does not mean one, and
person does not mean person. Christian teachers used
the word 'person' to mean a mask, a way of being, but
not a person in the sense that we now use the word.
St Augustine, though he used the word 'person', made
a famous qualification. He says that Father, Son and
Holy Spirit are three persons, 'not because that was
what we wanted to say, but so as not to be reduced to
silence'.[3]

Today the word 'person' carries with it connotations
of self-consciousness and denotes a distinct, self-aware
individual. This expanded use is misleading when we
speak of God as a person, simply because God is so
much more. We think of a person belonging in time
and space, able to sustain a limited number of deep
relationships, whose influence, though it may be extensive, eventually hits firm boundaries. To think of God
as a person implies that God is the same as us, only
more so – a kind of super-person. Our imagination then
has difficulty understanding how God can be present
simultaneously to the vast numbers of people praying
at any given moment. How can God hear, let alone
respond to tens of thousands of contradictory requests
every day?

Occasionally, people picture God using office equip-
ment to ease the burdens – originally books, but now,

of course, computers. Billy Graham has often used such pictures, but they only compound the difficulty, and give the impression that God is some kind of 'super-nerd'.

God graciously relates to us in personal ways, because we are people. But God is beyond our imagining. Even the best analogies are, as St Augustine says, merely 'footprints of the divine'. Most of the familiar pictures of God as father, mother, shepherd, king, hunter, lover and so on are human, personal images. There are others. Plato pictures God as the sun, shining in full strength, giving light and warmth and energy, unchanging, reliable; and in its light, we see light.

Jesus speaks of the Spirit as wind, a great energy which we cannot control, the breath of life, a gentle cooling breeze, and a terrifying and devastating tornado. The Spirit was given to the first disciples by the risen Jesus, as he breathed on them with the breath of new life; and as a rushing, mighty wind which filled the whole house on the day of Pentecost.

The pictures of wind and sun are not personal images, but they do convey something of the greatness and glory and power of God, and the fact that God is spiritual presence and power, everywhere and in all things. When we pray and ask God to make things happen, we are praying to the God who loves and cares and listens and speaks, who knows our needs before we ask. We are also praying to the God whose power is infinite, who holds the universe in being, whose 'never-failing providence ordereth all things, both in heaven and earth'.[4] Prayer reveals what we believe about God.[5]

Prayer also indicates what we think about ourselves in relation to God. On the face of it, prayers of petition make nonsense of a relationship with God. Such prayer provides reminders and requests to the God who knows our needs before we ask. It is prayer which too easily lapses into concentration on human needs, rather than on God's presence. The essence of a relationship with God is trust; yet in this kind of prayer, we bother God in a way which implies a lack of trust. Better, then, to abandon prayers of petition altogether, and concentrate on other, supposedly higher forms of prayer.

Yet requests of every kind, and encouragement to make such requests, are frequent in the New Testament. Petition is at the heart of prayer, because it focuses so sharply the personal nature of the relationship with God. A prayer of petition is, above all, an act of will, and it is in the exercise of our wills that we are most truly personal. When we decide to ask for this rather than that, when we make choices, when we ask for this person to be healed, when we use our will so that we are not mere items in a process of events, then we act as individual persons. Only so can we relate to other people.

When two people come to be married, they are about to enter into the most deeply personal of relationships. The law defines marriage as a 'voluntary' union, and the word 'voluntary' comes from the Latin *voluntas*, which means 'will'. Marriage must be entered into freely, as a deliberate act of will. If there is undue pressure, so that one or both of the people involved have no choice, then it is not a true marriage.

The first words which the bridegroom and the bride say in the marriage service are 'I will.' I attended a service on one occasion when the bridegroom had to be asked the same question three times. The third time it was asked in words rather different from the prescribed form. The priest looked straight at him and said, 'Are you going to say "I will" or not?' And the bridegroom took a deep breath and said, 'I will.' Without those words, the service would have come to a grinding halt.

The vows then give detailed substance to that act of will. In making the vows, and declaring their will, bride and groom are invited to act most truly as persons in relation to each other. They may, of course, be carried along on a tide of romantic feeling, or, worse, they may be getting married to please their relatives. But ideally, the words 'I will' say, in effect, 'I am me, and you are you, and I am making a deliberate and careful choice to give myself to you in the deepest of personal relationships.'

Prayers of petition lie at the heart of prayer because they are acts of will. In the mundane act of 'letting our requests be made known', we assume the high stature of persons in relationship with God. The prayer of being in God, of resting and of communion, prayers of worship and adoration and thanksgiving, are all forms of prayer which may confirm and strengthen a personal relationship with God. But, as H. H. Farmer comments, 'prayer must have act and will at the centre of it, must be more than a mere state of mind, if it is to be the relation of a self to God, a genuine personal relationship. The expression of such act and will, such selfhood even in the very presence of the Eternal, is petition.'[6]

Such prayer tells what we believe about God and what we think about ourselves. But does prayer make any real difference? How does God deal with such vast numbers of requests, which must frequently be contradictory? The question to which we most urgently want an answer is, Do our requests make any real difference to what actually happens? Is my friend more likely to survive his heart bypass operation, and to make a full recovery, because I am praying for him?

One of the reasons why Ludovic Kennedy said 'a farewell to God' was because prayer was not answered. Every Sunday morning, his father said the prayer for the Navy: 'O Eternal God, preserve us from the dangers of the sea and from the violence of the enemy . . .' until the day he died, when his ship was torpedoed. It was, he concluded, absurd to think that prayers to the Almighty could have any influence on the outcome of events.[7]

Three main suggestions about the influence that prayer might have are generally on offer. One is that prayer makes no difference at all to what happens, but does affect our relationship with God. A second is that in direct response to prayer, God changes the course of events. A third is that prayer makes no difference to what actually happens, but it does influence the way in which we think about it.

If prayer is above all the expression of a personal relationship, then we have to rid ourselves of mechanical and managerial pictures. To talk about God making certain things happen and not others implies that God is pulling levers and pressing buttons. To picture God sorting through the day's requests, and deciding which to act on and which to reject, is not particularly helpful.

Professor Galbraith was once subjected to a great deal of hate mail as a result of something he said, including vitriolic letters from people who assured him that they were beseeching the Almighty to cause him to lose either

life or limb, or, at the very least, the power of speech.
He wrote:

> 'I crawled into bed, reflecting with less than character-
> istic piety, on all the prayers that were spiralling up
> at that moment petitioning my dismemberment or
> destruction. I thought of saying a word on my own
> behalf and then struggled with the shattering thought
> that these matters might be decided by majority vote.[8]

There is no evidence that God conducts telephone polls,
and acts on the will of the majority. Mechanical or
managerial pictures are not appropriate. If we are to
make any sense of prayer and providence, we must think
in personal terms.

When I pray for a friend who is about to go into
hospital for a serious operation, there is a three-way
relationship, between me, the person I am praying for,
and God. My prayers may include the surgeons who
will operate, and the nurses in the high-dependency unit.
They will also embrace my friend's wife and his family.
As an act of will and as an expression of my love and
concern, I pray to God that my friend will come through
the operation and make a complete recovery.

John Baker suggests that the relationship established
by this prayer provides the means whereby God's Spirit
can reach the person for whom I am praying: 'God's
spirit needs a pathway ... and our human love and
concern, and our natural psychic networks with those
involved may supply that, if made available in love for
him to use.'[9]

It is an attractive suggestion, and one which makes

some sense of prayer. But it seems to me that there is no evidence to suggest that God 'needs' a pathway in order to reach someone else. God knows my friend's need better than I, and can reach him directly.

Perhaps there is a clue in Baker's use of the phrase 'natural psychic networks', which suggests that my prayer may release psychic and spiritual energy which could make a small but significant contribution to the healing process. But there is nothing exclusively Christian about this, and it is not necessarily related to prayer. It is a natural pattern of life and an experience which is not confined to those who have faith.

Laurens van der Post tells, in *The Seed and the Sower*, of a terrible time in a Japanese prisoner-of-war camp, when the guards were in the grip of a deep madness and every one of the prisoners was at risk. The spell was broken by one of the prisoners, a South African named Celliers, but at terrible cost to himself.

He had one brother, who was thousands of miles away in South Africa and did not even know that he had been captured. While Celliers was enduring a most dreadful, lingering death, his brother began to sing a song which both brothers had known in their childhood. His wife asked him why, and he said he felt that Celliers was in terrible trouble and needed him. For a week he thought of his brother with great intensity, and went around singing for him the song they both knew. At the same time, Celliers was dying, and crooning to himself, in a harsh, broken whisper, the same song that his brother was singing. After three days, Celliers died. On the same day, his brother stopped singing.[10]

A great many people experience this kind of

communication, and support one another by the release of spiritual and psychic energy. Celliers had no way of knowing that his brother was thinking of him with such love and intensity, and may not have been aware of it in his conscious mind. But the energy released for him helped him to die well, and in peace. Neither of the two brothers prayed; but the current of communication flowing between them and the release of energy are, for those with faith, gifts of God in creation.

God does not answer our prayers by causing things to happen which otherwise would not have happened; unless, of course, the answer is one of those exceptionally rare miraculous events. But the release of energy, and the focus provided by the prayer which is a specific request, may make a real difference to the outcome. My prayer for my friend who is about to undergo a major operation may mean that the skill of the surgeons and the nurses, the love and concern of the family, and his own will to recover are at their peak, and that may make the difference between life and death.

People going in to examinations sometimes pray. It is not unknown for such people to come out of the examination exclaiming delightedly, 'I prayed, and exactly the right questions came up – just the ones I'd revised for!' But do they seriously believe that God has ordered the setting of the paper, weeks in advance, to meet their needs; or has guided them in their revision to concentrate on specific topics? Apart from that, there will be other people emerging from the same exam, who have not prayed, and who are also delighted that the subjects they revised have come up. And there may be other people who also prayed, for whom the paper was a disaster.

The prayers have not changed either the content of the paper or the course of the revision. What they have done, properly understood, is to enable the person taking the exam to focus properly, to relax, and so to give of their best. In this sense, prayer has made a difference. The fruit of the Spirit may be found not only in love, joy and peace, but also in the ability to give ourselves completely to the task in hand.

'Whatever you do,' writes St Paul, 'in word or deed, do everything in the name of the Lord Jesus.'[11] In part, at least, that means giving ourselves wholly and completely to whatever we do, so that the potential in every situation, for us and for others, will be fully realised. Prayers of petition may help us, and other people, to do this, and so may make a real difference to what actually happens. But such prayers do not always have to be expressed in words.

There are people who give themselves so completely to the task in hand that they never manage to spend time in prayer. Possibly they have no inclination to, either. Or they simply cannot understand why prayers of petition are necessary and think they make little difference to what happens. John Taylor tells of receiving a letter from a Christian teacher working in a school in a remote part of Nigeria. She was concerned about five boys whose families could not afford to pay even the modest fees for the school. They were, she wrote, 'pretty constantly on my mind', though she did not pray for them specifically at all. Within a month, four had received financial help, and at Christmas time, the teacher received a gift to be used for any boy who was in need.

She saw these gifts as the direct result of God's concern, and added, 'I do not see that formal intercession would have made any difference one way or the other.' But when a person whose life is given to God has other people 'pretty constantly in mind', she is creating a three-way relationship between God, herself and the people in question. Her concern is her request, and she is helping to release that spiritual energy which makes a difference to what happens, even though her prayer never takes direct form. John Taylor comments that when someone whose life is simply and sacrificially dedicated to God has another human being 'pretty constantly in mind', that surely is the whole of intercession.[12]

Prayer can also have a profound effect on the way in which we think about what happens. It is sometimes said that answers to prayer are mere coincidence, and the pious answer to this is 'Maybe. But it is a curious fact that when a person stops praying, coincidences don't happen.' It is much more likely that the coincidences do still occur, but because they have not been prayed for, they are not noticed.

Prayer makes a difference to the way in which we look at life. I have suggested, through the experience of Celliers and his brother, that the release of energy through an intense awareness of and concern for other people is part of the pattern of life, and is a gift of God in creation.

Prayer makes the connections explicit, and links together, in a conscious and deliberate way, the person praying, the person prayed for, and God. The main difference between a Christian and a person who is not a

Christian is not that a Christian has experiences which a non-Christian does not have. The primary difference is that a Christian meets, in the ordinary experiences of life, that meaning and presence which is God. Prayer takes us behind the veil, and lets us see the hand of God in the ordinary experiences of life.

Prayer may also help us to accept the will of God when that will conflicts with ours. Prayer is an act of will in which we are most truly persons. Making our requests known to God is only possible because we are in a personal relationship; but it is a curious relationship in which one party always insists on their own way. Prayer is an act of faith, of trust in the will of God. It is an act of submission to a higher will and a greater purpose. Prayer is offered in the belief that God knows what is best for us, and in the conviction that 'in all things, God works together for good with those who love him'.

There is, of course, no guarantee that prayer will lead to a creative acceptance of whatever happens as the will of God. A girl of nine was seriously ill with leukaemia, and her mother prayed that she would recover. She did not add any qualifications to her prayer, such as 'if it be your will'. She could not believe that God wanted her daughter to die. She was sure that God's will was for her daughter to be well again. But her daughter died. So did the mother's faith.

If my friend dies in the course of his heart bypass operation, or shortly afterwards, his family and I will be deeply saddened, and puzzled that our prayers for his healing have not been answered. We may express that sadness and bewilderment, even anger, in our prayers. But the very fact that we have prayed and are praying may also help us to accept what has happened, to make something creative out of it, and to recognize that death is the only gateway to perfect healing.

If my friend comes through the operation, and is able to lead a normal life again, we will, I hope, remember to give thanks. There are a great many occasions in the Gospels when we are told that Jesus prayed, but we are given an indication of the words of only two of those prayers. One is a prayer of thanksgiving, and the other is the prayer in the Garden of Gethsemane.

The New Testament frequently encourages the making of requests to God, but more frequently reminds us to give thanks. Requests are to be made known 'with thanksgiving'. Every one of St Paul's letters begins with thanksgiving to God, apart from two; and to receive a letter from Paul which did not begin with thanksgiving was ominous, a sure sign that the church was in disgrace. 'I believe that nothing more reveals our shortcoming,' writes John Baillie, 'than the fact that our prayers of petition always outnumber our prayers of thanksgiving.'[13]

Some years ago, two schoolboys were sitting opposite a farm worker in a train compartment. The farm worker took out his sandwiches, and before eating them, paused to give thanks. The boys asked him what he was doing, and he explained. They were astonished. 'We never do that,' they said. 'So what do you do?' asked the farm worker, and the boys replied, 'We just get on and eat.' The farm worker thought for a moment, and then said, 'You mean, just like my pigs.'

A great Scottish preacher, Dr Alexander Whyte, used to say that dogs and pigs attack their food with greedy and unreflecting haste, but human beings will pause and give thanks to God; and in that pause, that moment of thanksgiving, our dignity as human beings is expressed.

Jesus took bread, and gave thanks. It was an act of thanksgiving both for the ordinary things of life, and for the fact that through those ordinary gifts, we may receive the bread of life. The saying of grace, which is part of the Eucharist in some churches, is a recognition of God's providence in nature and in human society: 'Blessed are you, Lord God of all creation. Through your goodness we have this bread to offer, which earth has given and human hands have made. It will be for us the bread of life.'[14]

The prayer in the Garden of Gethsemane, as it is recorded for us, contains no thanksgiving. It is a prayer of agonized despair. It is impossible for us to enter into that agony, not merely because its intensity is more than we can bear, but because we know the end of the story. Jesus could not have had any certainty about what God would do.

In the Garden, he was in the grip of terrible distress and naked fear. He was 'troubled and distressed'. He told his closest friends that his heart was 'overwhelmed with grief and ready to break. He fell on his face, and his sweat became as it were great drops of blood falling on the ground.' This is not the description of a man leaning piously on a rock and looking up to heaven in a calm and collected way. It is the prayer of a man who is near the edge.

The words of his prayer, briefly recorded, consist of an act of will and an act of faith, a request and an acceptance. 'Abba, Father, all things are possible to you.

97

Take this cup away from me: yet not my will, but yours.'[15] He hoped, and desired more passionately than almost anything else, that his request would be granted. But the one passion which exceeded his request was his acceptance of whatever God willed.

It is only St Mark who tells us that Jesus speaks to God using the Aramaic word, *Abba*. Surprisingly, this is the only time in the Gospels when the word is used, though this one time is an occasion of unique stress. The word was used at the time of Jesus by children addressing their parents, and also by disciples as a courtesy title for their rabbi. It does not really mean 'Daddy', since family relationships were different then. But it does imply an intimacy, a closer and more personal relationship than is conveyed by the more formal words normally used to address God.

The request that Jesus makes is an act of will. It is Jesus acting with the full stature of a human person, knowing what he wants, asserting the power to choose and to decide. He knows that his prayer can make a difference. All things are possible to God. He knows that if cause and effect continue in the way they have so far, then he faces crucifixion and a horrible death. 'Take this cup from me.'

Jesus wonders, 'Can this really be the will of God?' It is the first and only time when we hear Jesus say the words, 'Not my will but yours.' That may indicate that he is unsure of God's will, and needs to know that he has to tread the path of suffering, and that there is no alternative. Through the agony and the crying and the praying, he knows that he must suffer and die.

So the prayer makes no difference to what happens,

but it does make a difference to Jesus himself. 'Not my will but yours' may have been said, at first, through gritted teeth. It is harder, more blunt, than 'nevertheless not my will but thine be done'. But by the end of his long time of prayer, when he comes to wake the sleeping disciples, he is collected again, and has accepted the will of God.

That will is the refusal of his request. The will of God, his Father, is that Jesus must suffer and die. Later, Jesus is plunged into even greater despair. The way of obedience, the acceptance of God's will, has no meaning at all. 'My God, my God, why did you forsake me?' Can such awful suffering really be the will of God; and if so, what kind of God is this?

Some suggestions for reflection

The leader of an open-air holiday club asked the children to pray for a fine day on Friday, when there would be special activities. A five-year-old girl prayed that night for a fine day. Her mother explained that it might rain on Friday because God knew best, and anyway the flowers needed rain. The next night the child prayed again for a fine day on Friday; 'and about those flowers,' she added, 'don't worry about them – we'll water them ourselves'.

Which is easier and more helpful, to think of God as a person or as personal; and which is accurate and right?

Strange Design

'Prayer indicates what we think about ourselves in relation to God.' What does your prayer indicate?

Does prayer make a difference to what actually happens, or only to the way in which we think about what happens?

Chapter 6

'If There Is an Auschwitz . . .'

Beethoven went completely deaf. He could still write music, but he could not hear his music being performed. Jacqueline du Pre lost control of her body. She could still listen to recordings she had made, and could give master classes, but she could no longer play the cello. Iris Murdoch lost the use of her mind. Once a brilliant philosopher and a great novelist, she did not even know, towards the end of her life, that she had written twenty-seven books.

Such suffering appears so precisely directed that it can seem to be the result of deliberate cruelty. Iris Murdoch did not believe in God, partly because she could not reconcile the suffering and cruelty in the world with belief in a God of love. But she did understand profoundly the difference between good and bad. She believed passionately in goodness, and thought that religion had a useful place in sustaining goodness against evil.

After many years of living as a contented bachelor, C. S. Lewis married, and found deep happiness. However, shortly after this his wife died. Lewis, a deeply religious man stumbling through the darkness of bereavement, wondered whether God might be a cosmic sadist. He wrote:

A noble hunger, long unsatisfied, met at last its proper food, and almost instantly, the food was snatched away. Fate (or whatever it is) delights to produce a great capacity and then frustrate it. Beethoven went deaf. By our standards, a mean joke; the monkey trick of a spiteful imbecile.

He found no comfort, only terror, when kind friends told him that his wife was now safe in God's hands.

If so, she was in God's hands all the time, and I have seen what they did to her here. Do they suddenly become gentler to us the moment we are out of the body? And if so, why? If God's goodness is inconsistent with hurting us, then either God is not good, or there is no God: for in the only life we know, he hurts us beyond our worst fears and beyond all we can imagine.[1]

Suffering, particularly the suffering of children, presents the most severe challenge to the Christian belief that the whole world is in the hands of God, and that those hands are the hands of caring love. For me, as for countless others, the memorial in Jerusalem to the children who died in the Holocaust is an unspeakably sad and disturbing place. If there is an Auschwitz, it is said, there cannot be a God.

The dreadful suffering and the appalling evil of the Holocaust have provoked a great deal of sober reflection, in the course of which every conceivable approach to suffering has been considered. The Holocaust has led some to the conclusion that there is no God, while others have come to faith because of it. It has been attributed solely to human evil. Some have thought it a punishment for sin. Others have pointed to the heroic endurance and courage of the victims. Many are silent. And there is a measure of truth in each of these responses.

The silence of many is eloquent. It is not only the scale of the devastation, and the horror of it, but also the mystery, which is too deep for words. Partial answers, stumbling explanations, may be offered, but they do not touch the depths of what happened. A little light may be shed, but the darkness soon puts it out. There is no answer to the problem of suffering, and silence is a truer recognition of that hard fact than facile explanations.

In its most acute form, the problem of suffering is caused by faith. Those who think that the universe is governed by blind, pitiless indifference have to make the best of it, but there is no great philosophical problem. But those who believe that at the heart of the universe there is a loving, personal God have to attempt to reconcile that belief with the fact of terrible suffering. And there is no fully satisfying answer. Faith may provide a way of living through suffering, but much remains in mystery. The silence of many is an eloquent reminder of the limitations of human reason.

As a result of the Holocaust, some concluded that belief in God was simply absurd. But surprisingly, perhaps, a careful sample of Auschwitz survivors showed that only just over one in ten had completely lost faith in God because of the death camps; while one in twenty moved from atheism to faith in God. Many of the survivors thought it not right to blame God for the acts of human beings, though a significant number of survivors thought that nothing could excuse God for not having intervened to prevent the Holocaust. The haunting question 'Where was God?' still echoes around the death camps.

The problem of evil can be, and often is, easily summarized: God, if there is a God, is by definition all-powerful and perfectly good. A perfectly good God would not allow human beings, who are the objects of love, to experience evil and suffering. An all-powerful God could prevent evil and suffering. But human beings do experience evil and suffering. Therefore there is no God.

One answer to this problem, recently argued again by philosophers of religion, is that our understanding of good and evil is severely limited. We cannot see sufficiently clearly what ultimate good might justify temporary suffering. God might have greater good in store which we cannot imagine, and suffering which seems purposeless could be justified if only we could see further into the divine intention.

It is true that we live by faith, not by sight, and that God's ways are past finding out; but nonetheless, we have to deal with the world as we see it and as we experience it. To suggest that God allowed the terrible evil of the Holocaust in order that a greater good might result – a good which we do not experience and cannot imagine – stretches credulity too far.

At the opposite extreme are those who suggest that either God's power is limited or God's love is not perfect, or possibly both. 'This whole problem of suffering is solved', Spike Milligan once remarked, 'if you say that God is not perfect. He's a good, imperfect God.' But why should anyone believe in or trust such a God?

The more traditional answer to the problem of evil hinges on the reality of human freedom. The love and perfect goodness of God overflow into the created world. It is a world in which God invites, but does not compel, a response of love; and the creation of a world in which the free response of love is possible inevitably carries with it the possibility of evil and suffering. God could have created a world in which there was no evil and no suffering; but it would have been a very different world. Love, beauty, truth and goodness are possible only where there is true freedom, and freedom involves the possibility that people will choose hatred, ugliness, falsehood and evil.

There are large numbers of atheists, agnostics and religious people who affirm the reality of human freedom, and regard that freedom as being genuine and serious. Genuine, in that it is real freedom. It is not absolute freedom, since our choices are conditioned by our desires, by the values prevalent in our culture, our families and our schools, and by other considerations; but freedom is nonetheless real. It is also serious, since we can choose between good and bad, between love and hatred. It is the freedom to choose evil that lies at the root of a great deal of suffering, and it was the recognition of this that led a great many of the survivors of the Holocaust to say that people, and not God, were responsible.

The roots of the Holocaust run deep in human history, and especially in Christian history. Bitter conflict between church and synagogue was evident soon after the death of Jesus. When Jews were dominant in numbers and influence, they denied the central facts of the Christian faith and persecuted Christians. When Christians became dominant, they persecuted Jews. And since Christians have been dominant from the time of the Emperor Constantine, in the fourth century, that persecution has lasted a long time.

The destruction of Jerusalem, and especially of the Temple, by the Romans in AD 70, was interpreted in St Matthew's Gospel as a judgement on the Jewish people, and as a direct fulfilment of the words spoken to Pilate. When Pilate announced to the people, 'I am innocent of this man's blood,' they all replied, 'His blood be upon us and upon our children.'[2] Is it my imagination, or does St Matthew emphasize the word *all*?

St John's Gospel was written at a time when conflict between church and synagogue was intense. His Gospel has Jesus say to the Jews, 'You are of your father, the devil, and your will is to do your father's desires. He who is of God hears the words of God; the reason why you do not hear them is that you are not of God.'[3] It is more likely that such words were spoken in the severity of the conflict between the church and the synagogue, than that Jesus himself said them.

The Church of the early centuries held two beliefs about the Jews. One was that God was finished with them, that the Church had replaced the Temple, and Christians had replaced Jews as the new Israel. The other was that the Jews killed Christ. From the early Church, through the Middle Ages and the Reformation, and well into the twentieth century, Jews were marginalized, despised, hated and persecuted by Christians.

Since it is extremely painful to hear what was said,

one quotation will be sufficient, one among a great many which might have been chosen from any time between the first century and the twentieth. In the fourth century, Jews were described as 'murderers of the Lord, assassins of the prophets, rebels and detesters of God, they outrage the Law, resist grace, repudiate the faith of their father, companions of the Devil, accursed, detesters, enemies of all that is beautiful'.[4] And though it is hard to believe, worse parts of this quotation have been left out.

On to this ground, so long prepared by the Christian Church, Hitler had only to scatter the seed of his own rage and hatred, and the seed grew and produced a grotesque harvest. To this great fire, so carefully laid, Hitler and the Nazis put a torch. The flames burned furiously because of age-old hatred and prejudice; because of the co-operation of large numbers of people in industry, medicine, science and administration; because of the collaboration of people in many lands; and because of the indifference and acquiescence of ordinary people.

On this view, the Holocaust was caused by human hatred and human evil. A great deal of the suffering in Ireland has been caused by terrorist bombs, by punishment beatings, by religious bigotry, by political errors. Much of the agony of the Sudan is caused by civil war between north and south. The freedom to do good, the freedom to love, also carries with it the freedom to do evil and to hate.

Human evil is, however, sometimes compounded by the belief that the evil is done in the name of God and is justified as divine punishment. In the sixteenth century,

Martin Luther wrote words which have a dark reson-
ance in the twentieth. He reminds the Jews that their
city and Temple, their priesthood and sovereignty were
destroyed 1,460 years before:

> One dare not regard God as so cruel that he would
> punish his own people so long, so terribly, so unmer-
> cifully, and in addition keep silent, comforting them
> neither with words nor with deeds, and fixing no time
> limit and no end to it. Therefore this work of wrath
> is proof that the Jews, surely rejected by God, are no
> longer his people, and neither is he any longer their
> God.[5]

So Luther advocated the burning of synagogues, the
destruction of Jewish homes, and the expulsion of the
Jews from the Germanic lands 'for all time'.

There were, and still are, Jewish rabbis who, for different reasons, considered the Holocaust to be a divine
punishment. One of the traditional Jewish prayer books
says that 'because of our sins, all this has come upon
us'. There are orthodox Jews today who regard the
Holocaust as God's punishment for the failure of the
Jewish people to honour their solemn covenant with
God.

If even a few Jewish leaders regard the Holocaust in
this way, their views have to be respected. But two things
must be said. One is that the punishment, if such it was,
does seem grossly out of proportion to the evil. The
other is that it was European Jews, and particularly
Eastern European Jews, who were consumed, but not
British or American Jews; which suggests that even con-

sidered as a punishment, it was the arbitrary act of a tyrant god rather than the righteous act of the living God.

Suffering is undoubtedly caused or increased by the evil done by others, or the evil which is self-inflicted. But to describe this as punishment inflicted by God implies that God is cross, like an angry schoolmaster wielding a big stick; and the cliché, 'This will hurt me more than you' does not help. If God is perfect love, then God longs, with a strong and passionate longing, that we will live for goodness and truth and beauty. If we do not, if we choose not to, then God's love remains strong and passionate; but the idea that we then experience the reverse side of God's love – that love turns into wrath, and punishment, and possibly into everlasting punishment – is, to say the least, problematic.

First, there is the great difficulty of making meaningful connections between suffering, punishment and love. A hospital chaplain recently spoke with the parents of a child who was very seriously ill. His opening remark was, 'Now, which of you two has sinned?' Believe that all suffering is punishment, and there is logic in his remark; but it is an obscene kind of logic.

The prophets used to declare that as a punishment for sin, God had sent rain upon one city and not on another. We now know that in the skies between where those cities used to be, weather fronts meet. The occurrence of natural phenomena tells nothing about the righteousness of one community and the sin of another. It is particularly difficult to make meaningful connections when punishment falls upon the righteous and the wicked escape scot-free. The Psalms frequently lament the fact that the ungodly flourish like a green bay tree, while it is the faithful who suffer. These difficulties are an inevitable consequence of thinking that all suffering is caused, ultimately, by human sin; because if that is true, then no suffering is accidental, or misfortune, or bad luck.

Characteristically, what Jesus said about this is uncomfortable. People asked him about some Galileans, who just happened to be in the wrong place at the wrong time. They were offering sacrifice when Pilate had them killed. 'Were they sinners above all the other Galileans?' the people wanted to know; and Jesus answered, 'No.' And he reminded them of another incident, the sudden collapse of a tower at Siloam, which fell on eighteen people and killed them. 'No,' said Jesus, 'they were not worse offenders than everyone else in Jerusalem.' But to this reassuring 'No' he added the disturbing comment, 'but unless you repent, you will all perish.'

He did not say that these people were killed as a punishment for sin, nor that anyone else would be. But nor did he say what we want him to say – namely, that the people who died were innocent, and it was just an accident. Instead, he chose to remind us that we are all sinners, without exception, and that unless we repent, unless we change direction, we are all on the road to death.

The question which concerned the people echoes an anxiety which frequently disturbs those who suffer: 'What have I done to deserve this?' we ask. It is a question which carries with it the implied answer, 'Nothing.' With the notable exception of the suffering which people bring on themselves, the implied answer is probably true. But the words of Jesus are a salutary reminder that people who suffer have not done more than anyone else, but nor have they done less, to deserve it; that we are all sinners; and that we are all liable to suffer the consequences of living in a world which is seriously out of joint with the purposes if its creator.

Second, there is the difficulty that if God causes people to suffer as a punishment for their sins, then God is doing evil in order that good may come. However important the good may be, deliberately causing suffering remains an evil. God is often compared to parents who punish their children out of their deep love for them. Suffering is the equivalent of God shouting at us. Pain has been described as 'God's megaphone' to rouse a deaf world. 'No doubt,' writes C. S. Lewis, 'pain as God's megaphone is a terrible instrument; it may lead to final and unrepented rebellion. But it gives the only opportunity the bad man can have for amendment. It removes the veil; it plants the flag of truth within the fortress of a rebel soul.'[6]

It is important to distinguish between pain and suffering which are an integral and necessary part of the created world as the reverse side of love and goodness, and pain and suffering which are caused deliberately by God as a direct punishment for sin. It is, of course, true that there is what may be called retribution built into the created order. 'You reap what you sow.' The chances of an early and miserable death are greatly increased by regular smoking. But even this retribution is somewhat arbitrary. Many people smoke all their lives and suffer no serious ill effects.

It is one thing to create a world in which there is the

possibility of suffering, because that is bound up with the possibility of human freedom and the possibility of growth into maturity. It is quite another to cause pain as a punishment for sin, deliberately to do evil in the hope that good may result. The absolute love of God does not do evil.

There is, thirdly, the difficulty that, in traditional Christian theology, the fact that the righteous suffer in this world while the wicked flourish is resolved by a neat reversal of fortune in the next. Lazarus is carried by the angels into Abraham's bosom, while Dives is tormented in the fires of hell. But what are we saying about God when we believe that he condemns people to eternal torment as a punishment for evil, however great, which is committed over a limited period of time?

Jesus spoke about Gehenna, 'where their worm does not die and the fire is not quenched'. The people who heard him would have known that he was referring to the rubbish tips outside the city walls, where fires burned continually, while a particular kind of worm flourished just beneath the surface. The parable of Dives and Lazarus tells us nothing about the furniture of heaven or the temperature of hell. It tells one simple truth, with great power and vividness: that if people have the law of Moses in their hands and Lazarus on their doorstep, and do nothing at all to help him, then not even resurrection will move them.

One meaning of the word for 'judgement' in the New Testament is the word 'disintegration'. Shaw's vision of hell is of people following trivial pursuits for ever – an endless round of shopping, and then coming in to watch *Neighbours*, *Coronation Street* and *Brookside* (I deliberately leave out *Eastenders* because that's the one I watch!). In *The Great Divorce*, Lewis imagines Napoleon striding endlessly up and down a wonderfully decorated banqueting room, muttering to himself, 'It was all Josephine's fault.'

What is described as God's punishment, or wrath, may perhaps be better understood as God's passionate love and longing for us, from which we remove ourselves to our own great and everlasting cost. Christian faith does not teach that we are immortal, or that there is that in us which continues beyond death. Christian faith believes in resurrection; which may be dependent on there being some response to the love of God. Without that, there is nothing. I once asked a Jewish rabbi whether he thought Hitler was in hell. 'No,' he replied. 'No, I don't think so. Because I don't believe in that kind of God.'

Punishment, if it is understood as the consequence of abusing the laws of nature, or as a consequence of living in a world which is out of joint with God's purposes, may be a partial explanation for the fact of suffering. But what are we to say of the more commonly heard justification for suffering – that it results in nobility?

One of the greatest conductors of classical music in this century was Otto Klemperer. He was a victim of Hitler's rise to power, and was exiled from Germany. He suffered a brain tumour, which left him partially paralysed and in constant pain. Shortly after an operation to remove the tumour, he fell and broke his leg, and was unable to walk for years. He was once smoking in bed, and burning ash fell on the sheet. He reached for the water jug, grabbed the wrong one, and soaked himself in highly inflammable embrocation, which caused terrible burns.

All this he survived, and he continued conducting, searching more and more deeply into the very heart of music. 'A man who has been through as many hells as Otto Klemperer,' wrote Bernard Levin, 'comes out burned down to his soul's bones. He is an embodiment of the dangerous truth that suffering can ennoble.'

Not all suffering ennobles. It can, as easily, destroy. But there are a great many heroic examples of the remarkable truth that suffering can ennoble. It is a dangerous truth because it can be used to justify suffering; and great suffering does not become morally right because some people manage to rise above it. As John Baker tartly comments, 'It would make as much sense to say that, because Milton triumphed over his blindness to compose *Paradise Lost*, blinding people is the way to produce great epic poets.'[7]

The same argument applies to the belief that suffering may be justified if it produces good results. The Holocaust led to the creation of the state of Israel, though in the process further great wrong has been done to the Palestinians. The murder of Stephen Lawrence led to the Macpherson Inquiry and to a greater determination that Britain should become a genuinely non-racist society. But neither the murder of Stephen Lawrence nor the Holocaust could, by any stretch of the imagination, be considered good because an attempt was made to bring something good and creative out of them. Both events remain great evils.

Whether suffering is thought of as being due to human evil, or as punishment, or as an inevitable consequence of the abuse of the natural world, whether or not suffering ennobles or leads to good consequences, these are only candles flickering dimly in the darkness. When all has been said, there remains a great deal of suffering for which no explanation is remotely adequate. It brings us back to the basic problem: a God who is perfect love would not want people to suffer; a God who is all-powerful could prevent suffering; people do suffer; therefore there is either no God, or God's power is limited, or God's love is less than perfect.

The Christian belief is that God is all-powerful, all-knowing, and perfectly good. But this does not mean that God can do anything or that God knows everything. A schoolboy once asked a friend if God could make two and two into five, and received the crisp reply, 'Of course not. God doesn't do silly things like that.' Omnipotence means that God can do everything that does not involve a logical contradiction. God could not, for example, make people exist and not exist at the same time.

To suggest that God could create people who are both free and not free is a logical contradiction. If God creates free human beings, who have a genuine and serious choice between good and evil; if that is the only way in which love may be answered by love, then God must limit the use of that power which would control and direct the wills and affections of people. Power, we have already suggested, is shown most clearly in the ability to limit its use.

The frequent use of the word 'Almighty' in Christian worship may therefore be seriously misleading. It might be more truthful and more helpful to think of God as inviting, beckoning, enticing, even luring human beings into love and true humanity; but never using almighty power to drive, to force or to compel. The theologian John Macquarrie describes God's creative work as a three-fold process of *conferring* freedom, dignity and responsibility on human beings; of *sustaining* the created order of a moral universe, with all its possibilities; and of what he describes as *letting be*, which is not the careless 'Let's just see what turns out' but the positive and dynamic word which says, 'You have the freedom and resources: now *be*.' Letting be gives us the freedom and the beckoning invitation to see, and to become.

If it is true that God chooses to limit the use of almighty power, then it follows that one of the main limitations on the use of that power is not knowing what will happen. To say that God knows everything means that God knows everything that has happened, and everything that is happening, and everything that might happen; but it does not mean that God knows everything that will happen. If human freedom is genuine and serious, then God does not know in advance what our choices will be, and must respond to them as they are made. And if God did know in advance what choices we would make, and altered the course of events so that the more disastrous choices were avoided, that would mean that our freedom was just a sham.

It is, however, not entirely satisfactory to say, in regard to the Holocaust, that God did not know what choices people would make. For while that may be true of specific choices, God does know what might happen, and God could and should have foreseen the Holocaust and done something to prevent it. Some survivors of the Holocaust thought it inexcusable that God evidently did nothing. They found the silence of God terrible.

'If There Is an Auschwitz...'

There are really only two possible conclusions. Either there is no God; or, human freedom is so overwhelmingly important that God has chosen to limit the divine power to the great extent necessary to ensure that human freedom is genuine. God could have violated human freedom in order to prevent the Holocaust. God made the choice not to, a choice terrible in its consequences. One can only assume that the alternative, the violation of human freedom, would ultimately have been even worse.

But where was God, where is God, when people suffer? The traditional belief is that God does not suffer. Some of the earliest understandings of God, in Greek philosophy, concluded that God is above suffering and sympathy and feeling. For centuries traditional Christian belief held that God does not suffer. This did not mean that God was held to be indifferent to human concerns, or unconcerned; but it did mean that God could not be influenced or affected by the sufferings of human beings. God was thought of as wholly other, eternal, unchanging. To think of God suffering implied that God is like us, involved in the temporal world, liable to change, and subject to being acted upon. St Thomas Aquinas was careful to maintain that God does not suffer, and taught that in Christ, the one who is both human and divine suffers not as God, but as a human being.

Yet there was always something strange about the firm belief that God cannot suffer, which does not fit with the birth and life and death of Jesus. There is an incident in Helen Wadell's biography of Peter Abelard, the eleventh-century theologian, where Abelard and his friend Thibault find a rabbit caught in a trap, and as soon as they release it, the rabbit dies. It is Thibault who suggests that in the suffering even of one rabbit, God suffers too.

'Then, Thibault,' Abelard said slowly, 'you think that all this' – he looked at the little quiet body in his arms – 'all the pain of the world, was Christ's cross?' 'God's cross,' said Thibault. 'And it goes on.' 'Heresy,' muttered Abelard mechanically, 'But, O God, if it were true.'[8]

For many people today, it is true that God suffers. God is described as *The Crucified God*. It is not only Christ, as a human being, who suffers on the cross, but God suffers in Christ. God is now described as the great companion, the fellow sufferer who understands.

It is scarcely possible to love someone fully, as God loves, without sharing deeply in their joy and in their sorrows. Perfect love is bound to suffer, and would not be perfect if it did not. God is present in the world, vulnerable, grieving, suffering, rejoicing. God suffers with us. But God is other, eternal, the creator of all that is. Unlike us, God can suffer without ever being overwhelmed by it.

It is sometimes held that the way to help someone who suffers is to serve as 'a bottomless pit'. At a particularly difficult time, I was once told that; and while I appreciated the offer of an infinite capacity to absorb whatever I said, without judging, it also made me deeply insecure. A 'bottomless pit' means that you keep on falling. God does not offer the kind of understanding and sympathy which goes on falling with you, because 'underneath are the everlasting arms'. God is not only 'the fellow sufferer who understands', but also the living God who sustains and transforms.

God is not only in Christ on the cross, suffering with him and in him. God is also the living God, creator and sustainer of the whole universe, suffering in Christ in order to fulfil the great purposes of divine love. The cross was an event in history, in which God suffered with us and for us. It is also an event for all time, which shows us what God is always like.

In the cross of Christ, there are all the different elements in suffering which we have considered in this chapter. There is the long and dreadful silence, darkness over all the land from the third hour until the sixth hour. There is the suffering caused by human sinfulness, the mistaken idealism of Judas, the weakness and fear of the disciples, the political expediency of Caiaphas, the line of least resistance taken by Pilate. There is the idea of suffering as punishment, given particular force by the belief that God's curse falls on anyone who is hanged on a tree. There is the desolating emptiness of feeling that God is silent, unconcerned, remote, or powerless. 'My God, my God, why did you forsake me?'

There is also nobility in the suffering of Christ. From the time of the arrest to the moment of his death, Jesus accepts his suffering, not with fatalistic submission, but with the strong belief that, despite all the evidence to the contrary, he is doing the will of God. His trust in God's providence does not falter. At the end of it all, he utters the goodnight prayer of every Jewish child, 'Father, into your hands I commit my spirit.'

Some suggestions for reflection

'*Christianity asks us to concentrate our attention upon barbarism, upon a barbaric pain and a barbaric act. Those crucifixes and crosses are symbols of horrendous cruelty and desolation and pain. It is not possible to make a journey through this life without experiencing grief, pain, all sorts of anguish. It seems inseparable from our knowledge of what it is to be a human being. That knowledge gives us freedom.*' (Dennis Potter)

In what ways does faith make the problem of suffering most acute?

Do the consequences of suffering ever justify the reality of suffering?

Can God still be God if God does not know everything that will happen?

Chapter 7

Just and Gentle Rule

It is hard to believe now, but there was a time when people believed in the steady march of human progress. The advance of science in particular promised that the new Jerusalem would be established on earth, if not in the immediate future, then within the next century, and certainly by the new millennium.

All such hopes were soon extinguished. Writing about 1914, John Buchan said that 'Everywhere in the world was heard the sound of things breaking.' The First World War, the slaughter of millions in the trenches, followed by the death of millions more in a flu epidemic which science was powerless to contain; the long years of the depression; the Second World War, the Holocaust, and the dropping of atomic bombs; civil wars, widespread famine and Aids; all this has given the twentieth century a strong claim to the dubious distinction of being the worst in human history.

In the face of this, extravagant hopes about human progress in the new millennium sound like facile optimism. We know what we are capable of inflicting upon one another. We know that science and technology are always ambiguous, and can be used both for healing and for destruction. Human nature does not change because one millennium gives way to another.

In the nineteenth century, 'progress' used to be a word full of hope. Progress promised a better life, for everyone. In the course of the twentieth century, progress has become the fate to which we feel ourselves condemned. What will it become in the twenty-first century?

For we also know that we are capable of generous and gentle goodness, as well as of wonderful achievements in art, science and technology. The advances made by human beings and by society in the past hundred years are almost as remarkable as the return to barbarism. So what of the future? We have considered providence in relation to history, nature and personal life; and we have taken seriously the reality of human freedom, evil and suffering. Christian faith holds that the future is with God too, and that the immediate future as well as eternity are held in God's good providence.

Predicting the immediate future is hazardous, to say the least. But even if we do not know what will happen, we do know the major issues which confront us and what we have to do. We have to care for the earth, urgently, before we pollute the world to an extent which will be quite literally fatal. We have to make intelligent decisions about the way in which we use the power we now have, particularly the power over birth and death. And we have to learn to use the astounding advances in information technology to communicate with one another, and to organize society in a way which makes people feel that they matter. The environment, the control of science, and human responsibility in one world, are, in my view, the most pressing issues; and amidst the dire warnings and the predictions of gloom, there are small but hopeful signs.

Just and Gentle Rule

The one thing that is certain in the future is that substantial advances in science and technology will be made. But what matters most in a technological society is not what we can do, but how we think about what we can do, and whether we can exercise control over it in the interests of goodness and humanity. Thomas Merton wrote:

> Taken by themselves, the achievements of technology are magnificent. But the Greeks believed that when a man had too much power for his own good, the gods ruined him by helping him to increase his power at the expense of wisdom, prudence, temperance and humanity.[1]

A famous and revealing comment was made by the philosopher Descartes, who died in 1650. The aim of science, he declared, was to make human beings 'the masters and possessors of nature'. Knowledge is power, and by increasing knowledge, human beings would be able to exercise ever greater control over the natural world. This, it was thought, was the way to live up to the image of God, by possessing and using power over the created world. In 1965, Merton wrote:

> The central problem of the modern world is the complete emancipation and autonomy of the technological mind, at a time when unlimited possibilities lie open to it, and all the resources seem to be at hand. Indeed, the mere fact of questioning this emancipation, this autonomy, is the number one blasphemy, the unforgivable sin in the eyes of modern man, whose

faith begins with this: science can do everything it likes, science must be permitted to do everything it likes, all that is done by science is right. Technology and science are now responsible to no power and submit to no control other than their own.[2]

There is today a widespread ambivalence towards the achievements of science. On the one hand, we are glad to accept the benefits. Some years ago, at the start of the heart transplant programme, Bernard Levin fulminated against this latest scientific advance. The prospect of having his failing parts replaced one by one did not appeal to him, and he rejected vigorously the fatalistic attitude that if we can do it, we should, and probably will. Today, heart transplants are a matter of routine for which large numbers of people are profoundly thankful.

On the other hand, there is a feeling that things are getting out of hand, that it has all gone too far, and that we are somehow overreaching ourselves. 'In twenty years time,' predicts Germaine Greer, 'women who have children naturally will be a small minority, the earth mothers, and they will be laughed at.'[3] Technically it is possible now for a couple, committed to their work, to have a child who is genetically theirs, but is carried by a surrogate mother, so that their careers are uninterrupted; or, if they prefer, they could use a donor so as to have a child with particular looks and abilities, and of the gender they choose. We can change the genetic structure of plants, but we cannot yet see where it will all end. Perhaps it would be best to call a halt now before it all gets completely out of hand.

Technically, we can share knowledge and information

on an unprecedented scale and with great speed, opening up vast opportunities. We can also share pornography on the same scale, and we can 'communicate' with one another without making any direct personal contact. Again, there are people who say that it has all gone too far, and who would, if they could, return to the age of quill pens and messengers on bikes.

The religious expression of this fear draws a clear line between God's territory and ours. A Member of Parliament who is a Christian objected strongly to parents being able to select the gender of their next child. For parents to make such a choice would, he thought, be a serious and unjustifiable intrusion into the work of the creator God. In other words, whether your next child is a boy or a girl is God's business, not yours. There are areas of life reserved to the divine providence, where we interfere at our peril. It is not given to us to control everything. Chance and randomness are an integral and essential part of the created order, and the more we control, the less we leave to chance. 'God moves in a mysterious way', and it is not given to us to penetrate, let alone order that mystery. It is wrong, possibly dangerous, even to make the attempt.

There are two problems with this. One is that it is a response of fear, and is therefore arbitrary. The line is drawn at the precise point where fear strikes, and when fear abates, the line is moved. More seriously, intelligent Christian faith does not respond to scientific advance by putting up boundary posts between God's territory and ours. It does not need to preserve a random element in nature lest without it there might be no space for God. When it is true to itself, Christian faith welcomes new knowledge because it tells us more about God's creative work and gives us more opportunity to participate with God in the world. The Christian response to scientific advance is to welcome it, and then to decide how to use the power and control that it gives us in the interests of true humanity.

A few years ago, three people met in a television studio. One was Louise Brown, the first 'test-tube baby', who was born in 1978. Another was the one thousandth 'test-tube baby'. And the third was Dr Patrick Steptoe, who was the first doctor to achieve successful *in vitro* fertilization. Louise Brown was asked if she knew what Dr Steptoe had done for her, and she replied, 'He made me.' Then she giggled, realising that was not quite right. Her spontaneous answer lies on one side of a great gulf, and her reflective giggle on the other. Does modern technology assist the natural processes of creation, or do we think that we can turn creation into a technological operation which is entirely under our control? It is one thing to assist the natural processes of creation, and to work in partnership with the creator God; quite another to think that we are in charge, and one day will control everything.

Louise Brown's birth was a technological triumph, but the techniques which made it possible were not regulated by law in any way. Technology, as Merton rightly said, 'submitted to no power and no control other than its own'. The Warnock Committee was not appointed until 1982, 'to examine the social, ethical and legal implications of recent and potential developments in the field of human assisted reproduction'. The committee reported in 1984. There was then a long period of discussion, sometimes very heated. Dame Mary Warnock commented on the abuse to which members of the Inquiry were subjected, both during their work and after the publication of their report.

The debate revealed on one side a heartless lack of compassion for childless couples, for the children who suffer from genetic disorders, and for their parents. It also revealed, on the other side, a chilling lack of respect for the human embryo. In the course of the debate, Members of Parliament were subjected to all kinds of lobbying. Dame Mary Warnock expressed considerable frustration at the length of time it took to give effect to her recommendations, but when the Act was eventually published, she changed her mind, recognizing that the long debate had allowed a consensus to develop.

In 1990, the Human Fertilization and Embryology Act was passed. It allowed certain treatments for infertility which involve the use of donors. It also, more controversially, allowed experiments on human embryos up to fourteen days, under certain stringent conditions. The Human Fertilization and Embryology Authority, set up under the Act, is responsible for licensing and regulating all centres in the UK which carry out fertility treatments involving the use of donors, storage of eggs, sperm and embryos, and research on human embryos.

Some years ago, there were proposals for a gender clinic in North London where, for £650, people would be able to choose the sex of their next child. The Authority issued a consultation document on Sex Selection. It considered the 'slippery slope' arguments, and the fears of people who worry about where it will all end. 'It is possible', says the document, 'to draw a line permitting some activities and prohibiting others. Devising and enforcing rules to achieve this is a principal role of the HFEA.' After the consultation, the Authority issued a code of practice, allowing sex selection for medical but not for social reasons. If there is a genetic disorder which is passed through the male line, then sex selection is allowed so that only girls are born; but it is not lawful for a landowner to use sex selection because he prefers a son to inherit his property.

When Diane Blood wanted to have a child, using sperm taken from her husband who had died, it was the HFEA which took the unpopular course of opposing it, on the grounds that the husband had not given informed consent. After she had appealed and won, the medical procedure had to be carried out abroad, because the HFEA had not licensed any clinic in Britain to act without consent. And when the child was born, the regulations were tightened up to ensure that respect for the individual, which is what informed consent means, would be surer in future.

It is the Human Fertilization and Embryology Authority which now provides a hopeful answer to the fears expressed by Thomas Merton in the 1960s. Scientists working in this field are no longer autonomous. Science and technology are subject to a power and a control other than their own. Society is not in the grip of a ferocious and all-consuming monster called scientific progress. We are in control. The HFEA, which we have set up, bears eloquent and reassuring witness to that fact.

The power to which scientists are subject is, of course, the law; and the control is set at the point which politicians judge to be the consensus which society has reached. Society is now largely secular, with a diminishing deposit of Christian values. The consensus which society reaches may not, in the view of Christians, be right, and it is the responsibility of Christians to work and to pray for a consensus which more accurately reflects what they believe to be the will of God.

Opinions differ, especially among Christians, on what the will of God is, which complicates the discussion and diminishes Christian influence. Some Christians hold that experimenting on human embryos up to fourteen days is justified, because the embryo is not capable of feeling pain, because a large number are lost naturally and fail to implant in the womb, and because the benefits of experimenting outweigh the harm done. Others hold that from the moment of conception, a human being exists, that to experiment on a human being without their consent is wrong, and that all life, including the human embryo, is sacred.

The divine providence does not make public announcements about what is right or wrong. We have to work in partnership with God and with one another to discover, using reason, intuition and all the resources of the tradition, what is right. But belief in God does mean that there is a wisdom and a standard of right and wrong which lies outside ourselves, and to which we are subject. It does not mean that whatever any individual happens to want is right for them, and should be allowed.

In the crucial questions affecting the beginnings of human life, we are seeking to discover and to do what is right, and we are choosing to limit the power we have gained to control and direct human reproduction. To me, that is a most hopeful sign, and a pointer to what we need to do in caring for the creation as a whole. We can, if we choose, work in partnership with God and with one another to use power in ways which enhance our humanity; but if we are to do that in relation to the creation as a whole, we must change the way in which we think about the world and God and ourselves.

For generations, human beings have been guided by the commission recorded in the first of the creation stories in the book of Genesis: 'Be fruitful and multiply and fill the earth and subdue it, and have dominion . . .'[4] When food was scarce, medicine primitive, and human beings had little knowledge of or control over nature, dominion was a worthwhile goal. Survival depended on it. Now that we have achieved such a large measure of control over the environment, we need to recognize that in the Bible and in Christian tradition there are other elements which have been seriously neglected. There is now far more emphasis on the story from the second chapter of the book of Genesis, which tells of the creation of man 'from the dust of the earth', and where the commission given is not to have dominion, but to 'till and tend' the earth.[5]

The emphasis is no longer on human beings gaining power over the earth, but on the fact that we are part of the created order, that we live or die by our care of the environment, and that we gain knowledge and power not in order to do things to the world, but in order to participate responsibly in the care of the earth. Human beings used to claim to be the crown of God's creation; but the climax of creation in the biblical narratives is the Sabbath. The crown of creation is God and the world and human beings enjoying each other on a day of being together in complete harmony.

Creation in the stories in Genesis is now seen to be not an act of power by an almighty God, so much as the expression of the being of God. The word of creation is parallel to the word of the incarnation. Process theology talks about God luring the world into being. Feminist theology speaks of God giving birth to the world. The world is not the plaything or the object of a transcendent God who does things to it, but is an expression of the being of God, who is at once wholly other and nearer than our very breath. Everything is in God, and the whole universe is sacramental.

Celtic spirituality in particular has always emphasized the divine presence in the whole of creation. There is a long tradition of Welsh literature which weaves nature and grace into a seamless robe of poetic beauty, linking the Eucharist and the created order. In the fourteenth century, Dafydd ap Gwilym wrote a poem called 'The Woodland Mass', in which the Eucharist is experienced 'in a birch grove in the sweet woods':

> There was here, by the great God,
> Nothing but gold in the altar's canopy.
> I heard, in polished language,
> A long and faultless chanting,
> An unhesitating reading to the people
> Of a gospel without mumbling;
> The elevation, on the hill for us there,
> Of a good leaf for a holy wafer.
> Then the slim eloquent nightingale
> From the corner of a grove nearby,

> Poetess of the valley, sings to the many
> The Sanctus bell in lively whistling.
> The sacrifice is raised
> Up to the sky above the bush,
> Devotion to God the Father,
> The chalice of ecstasy and love.[6]

Saunders Lewis wrote a poem in the same style for Ascension Day, but because he is a twentieth-century poet, he knows that nature is no longer as pure as it once was, and that people must come out of their little boxes (the council houses of verse three) if they are to see the glory of God:

> What's on this May morning in the hills?
> Look at them, at the gold of the broom and
>   laburnum
> And the bright surplice on the shoulders of the
>   thorn
> And the intent emerald of the grass and the still
>   calves.
>
> See the candlestick of the chestnut tree alight,
> The groves kneeling and the mute birch a nun,
> The cuckoo's two-notes over the shining bush of
>   the brook
> And the form of the mist bending from the censer
>   of the meadows.
>
> Come out, you men, from the council houses before
> The rabbits scamper, come with the weasel to see
> The elevation of the unblemished host
> And the Father kissing the Son in the white dew.

Lewis once remarked that 'The mass makes sense of everything', an early anticipation of that growing understanding which sees in the Christian Eucharist a way of valuing the created order. In the words of another twentieth-century poet, Gwenallt, Welsh spirituality 'makes sensuous the glories of God'.

In his book, *Paths in Spirituality*, John Macquarrie suggests that it is Celtic spirituality which provides the model for an authentic contemporary spirituality. 'At the very centre of this type of spirituality was an intense sense of presence ... but this presence was always mediated through some finite this-worldly reality, so that it would be difficult to imagine a spirituality more down to earth.' Welsh people today, who are aware of that presence in their own country, would question Macquarrie's use of the past tense.[7]

The resurrection of Jesus was experienced, first of all, as the presence of God. Later reflection recognized it as a great act of God's power, but it was as presence that the risen Jesus was first known. He was present with Mary in the Garden, with two people on their way home, with the disciples in the upper room and again at the lakeside.

The one thing about the resurrection which can be established by the normal methods of historical enquiry is that the first disciples were changed from being frightened, sad and disillusioned into people who were joyful, confident and courageous; and they said it was because of the presence of the risen Christ. It is the cross and the resurrection which show us what God is always like, and which are the strongest basis for Christian belief in divine providence, both now and in the future.

It is not possible for us now to hear the account of the death of Jesus and to know it for the first time. We have read the last chapter. We know in advance how the story ends. We assume, perhaps too readily, that Jesus too knew how it would all end. Did he not predict – it is, after all, recorded three times in the Gospel – that the Son of Man must suffer, and after three days, rise again? But even if Jesus himself said those words, even if they were not written into the account after the event, they were still an act of faith. Jesus had no way of knowing for certain that he would be raised from death.

The different words with which the four Gospels mark his death indicate that the disciples did not really know what he was thinking at the moment of death. Matthew and Mark give us the dreadful cry of dereliction as his last words, 'My God, my God, why did you forsake me?' Both tell us that he gave a loud cry before he died, but it is John who gives us the word of that cry. It was just one word, 'Finished.' It means, literally, 'It has been perfectly done.' Luke tells us that Jesus died with the quiet words of the Jewish goodnight prayer on his lips: 'Father, into your hands I commit my spirit.'

Jesus did not know how it would all end. His death was an experience of agonized despair, and of fulfilment, and of trust. He hoped and prayed and trusted that God would have the last word. In the end, in ways which he may or may not have imagined, his faith was vindicated. It is sometimes said that God always has the last word, and that the resurrection of Christ is the supreme example. In one sense that is true. The resurrection of Christ is God's victory, the last word which breaks the power of sin and death. The power of evil has to extend itself to its furthest limits in order to secure the suffering and death of Jesus; and even the worst evil cannot obliterate the presence of God. By raising Christ from the dead, God has the last word. But the deeper truth is that the resurrection is the first word of God's new creation.

Gerald Durrell tells of an incident when he was about ten years old, lying beside a sluggish stream in Greece, when a strange-looking insect crawled out of the water. It had thin legs, bulbous eyes, and a carunculated body, and it clung precariously to the stalk of a bulrush. Then it split down the centre of its back, and a crumpled creature struggled out, and clung to the stalk. For about ten minutes it dried out and slowly stretched in the sun, and then it whirred its wings and a beautiful dragonfly flew away. 'I had never seen such a transformation before,' says Durrell, 'and I gazed with wonder at the husk which had housed the beautiful shining dragonfly.'

The word 'transformation' is the same as the Greek word *metamorphosis*, and that is the word which is used to describe the transfiguration of Jesus. The resurrection was another transfiguration, this time complete and permanent. The body of Jesus was real and recognizable, but it was also changed, new, independent of time and space. 'Touch me, handle me,' invites Jesus, when the disciples are terrified that he is a disembodied spirit. They come to accept that he is somehow real, they know him and can recognize him.

Yet he is not the same. The resurrection is not the resuscitation of a corpse, a 'conjuring trick with bones', as Bishop David Jenkins so graphically put it. It is a transfiguration. If Jesus had appeared to the disciples in the same state that he was in at the time of his death

– battered, horribly wounded – they would have been appalled. Somehow, he had been changed. They were glad when they saw him. Yet they did not always recognize him at first. He was there with them one moment, and then gone. They were in a locked room and suddenly Jesus was in their midst. In the accounts in the Gospels, the disciples tell us that the risen Jesus has been transfigured.

The resurrection of Jesus is the first-fruit of the harvest, the first to be picked, which shows what the rest will be like. His resurrection body gives substance to that mysterious phrase in the creed about the resurrection of the body. C. S. Lewis writes:

> These small and perishable bodies we now have were given to us as ponies are given to schoolboys. We must learn the discipline of riding: not that we may some day be free of horses altogether but that some day we may ride bare-back, confident and rejoicing, those greater mounts, those winged, shining and world-shaking horses which perhaps even now expect us with impatience, pawing and snorting in the King's stables. Not that the gallop would be of any value, unless it were a gallop with the King; but how else, since he has retained his own charger, should we accompany him?[8]

The resurrection of Jesus also means that the last things are in the process of being realised. The Christian hope is that in the providence of God, love and goodness and truth are eternal; and the fact that evil was not able to destroy the love of Christ provides some basis in history for this hope. History is littered with the mistaken beliefs of those who predicted the actual date when Jesus would return, and would herald the end of the world as we know it. The dates come and go, and people either admit that they were wrong, or, more frequently, revise their predictions.

What is generally referred to as the second coming of Jesus stands for the truth that one day everything will be subject to the just and gentle rule of Christ. When that will be, and how it will be, are not given to us to know. Confident predictions that it will be linked in some way with the Millennium may or may not be mistaken. No one knows. What we do know is that God's love and care embrace everyone, that 'all things work together for good with those who love God', and that 'there is nothing in all creation that can separate us from the love of Christ.'[9]

Some suggestions for reflection

The creation itself will be set free from its bondage to decay and obtain the glorious liberty of the children of God ... for in this hope we were saved. (Romans 8:21,24)

Is it right to say that what matters most today is not what we can do, but how we think about what we can do; and if so, what are the implications of this?

What does the commission in Genesis 1:28 to 'be fruitful and multiply and fill the earth and subdue it, and have dominion over every living thing that moves upon the earth' mean for us today?

Can you discern any 'signs of the times' (Matthew 16:1–4), any indications that the whole world will one day be subject to the just and gentle rule of Christ?

Notes

Introduction

1. Norman Davies, *Europe, A History* (Oxford University Press, 1996), p. 897.
2. 2 Corinthians 5:17.
3. Job 26:14.

Chapter 1: The Accidents of History

1. I am indebted in this chapter to Sir Isaiah Berlin's essay on 'Historical Inevitability' in *Four Essays on Freedom* (Oxford University Press, 1969).
2. C. P. Snow, *The New Men* (Penguin, 1959), p. 123.
3. C. P. Snow, *Corridors of Power* (Penguin, 1966), p. 286.
4. David Thomson, *England in the Twentieth Century* (Pelican, 1965), p. 50.
5. This illustration assumes that either God's power or knowledge, or both, may be limited, and there is a fuller discussion of this in Chapter 6.
6. Genesis 45:5.
7. Genesis 50:20.
8. G. M. Trevelyan, *English Social History* 2 (Longmans, 1994), p. 125.
9. Ibid., p. 129.

10. Norman Davies, *Europe, A History* (Oxford University Press, 1996), p. 534.
11. Trevelyan, op. cit., p. 109.
12. A. Suggate, *William Temple and Christian Social Ethics Today* (T. & T. Clark, 1987), p. 177.
13. Alan Wilkinson, *Dissent or Conform?* (SCM, 1986), p. 92.
14. *The Voice of Winston Churchill* (Decca LXT6200).
15. BBC Archives LP29286.
16. Quoted in J. Baillie, *The Sense of the Presence of God* (Oxford University Press, 1962), p. 213.
17. Galatians 4:4.
18. C. F. D. Moule, *An Idiom Book of New Testament Greek* (Cambridge University Press, 1959), p. 1.

Chapter 2: Why a Bee Dances

1. Matthew 10:29.
2. Richard Dawkins, *River out of Eden* (Weidenfeld, 1995), p. 133.
3. A. Desmond and J. Moore, *Darwin* (Michael Joseph, 1991), p. 528.
4. Ibid., chapter 44.
5. Ed Carey, *The Faber Book of Science* (Faber, 1995), p. 498.
6. J. Baillie, *The Sense of the Presence of God* (Oxford University Press, 1962), p. 224.
7. Ibid., p. 221.
8. Ibid., p. 224.
9. Carey, op. cit., p. 504.
10. Ibid., p. 502.
11. Quoted from Radio 4.
12. Tennyson, *In Memoriam* LVI.
13. Romans 1:20.

Notes

14. Ephesians 4:13.
15. C. S. Lewis, *A Grief Observed* (Bles, 1961), p. 18.
16. Matthew 5:48, 30; Luke 10:27; 9:24.

Chapter 3: Did Jesus Find Me a Parking Space?

1. BBC Archives BLN20GV1778.
2. Romans 8:28.
3. 2 Corinthians 12:9.
4. Wendy Cope, *Serious Concerns* (Faber, 1992), p. 62.
5. Plato, *Laws* 902d–903a.
6. Matthew 10:29–30.
7. Genesis 12:1.
8. C. S. Lewis, *Miracles* (Bles, 1947), p. 208.
9. Job 1:21.

Chapter 4: It's a Miracle!

1. Mark 8:11–12; John 6:26–27.
2. *Crusade Magazine* (October 1976).
3. John 11:39.
4. Matthew 17:24–27.
5. John Baker, *The Faith of a Christian* (DLT, 1996), p. 57.
6. John 6:31.
7. John 6:35.
8. John 6:51.
9. E. B. Browning, *Aurora Leigh*, Book vii.

Chapter 5: 'Take This Cup From Me . . .'

1. Philippians 4:6.
2. 1 Kings 18:27.
3. *De trinitate* 5, 10
4. Prayer Book Collect for the Eighth Sunday after Trinity.

5. Cf. P. Baelz, *Prayer and Providence* (SCM, 1968), ch. 1.
6. H. H. Farmer, *The World and God* (Nisbet, 1935), p. 135.
7. Ludovic Kennedy, *All in the mind: a farewell to God* (Hodder, 1998).
8. J. K. Galbraith, *The Great Crash 1929* (Penguin, 1954), p. 17.
9. John Baker, *The Faith of a Christian* (DLT, 1996), p. 161.
10. L. van der Post, *The Seed and the Sower* (Penguin, 1963), ch. 6.
11. Colossians 3:17.
12. John Taylor, *The Go-Between God* (SCM, 1972), p. 242.
13. J. Baillie, *The Sense of the Presence of God* (Oxford University Press, 1962), p. 238.
14. *An Alternative Order for the Holy Eucharist*, (Church in Wales Publications, 1994), p. 29.
15. Mark 14:36.

Chapter 6: 'If There Is an Auschwitz . . .'

1. C. S. Lewis, *A Grief Observed* (Faber, 1961), p. 24.
2. Matthew 27:24–25.
3. John 8:42–46.
4. R. L. Rubenstein and J. K. Roth, *Approches to Auschwitz* (SCM, 1987), p. 48.
5. Ibid., p. 56.
6. C. S. Lewis, *The Problem of Pain* (Bles, 1940), p. 83.
7. John Baker, *The Faith of a Christian* (DLT, 1996), p. 117.
8. Helen Waddell, *Peter Abelard* (Pan, 1952), p. 212.

Notes

Chapter 7: Just and Gentle Rule

1. Thomas Merton, *Conjectures of a Guilty Bystander* (Sheldon, 1977), p. 69.
2. Ibid., p. 72.
3. BBC TV profile (March 1999).
4. Genesis 1:28.
5. Genesis 2:7–15.
6. From a paper prepared for St George's House, Windsor, by James Coutts on 'The Sacramental basis of Gwladgarwch'.
7. John Macquarrie, *Paths in Spirituality* (SCM, 1972), p. 122.
8. C. S. Lewis, *Miracles* (Bles, 1947), p. 195.
9. Romans 8:28, 38–39.